The Jazz Preacher

David Baroni

This, my first book, is dedicated with love and gratitude to my wife Rita. Thank you for being my friend, companion and partner in this adventure of life. I look forward to living many more chapters with you!

A big thank you to the friends we have made as we have traveled all over the world- your smiles and encouragement have meant more than you could imagine.

Thanks also to my daughters- Bethany, Charity, and Celeste- and my "son-in-grace", Ben, for laughing at my jokes. I also want to thank Bethany and Rhonda Rush for editing and helping with the manuscript.

"The Jazz Preacher"
David Baroni
First Printing 9/2007
Copyright: davidbaroni.com
All Rights Reserved

-1-
<u>Beginnings</u>

On a high bluff overlooking the mighty Mississippi River rests the sleepy, charming, historical town of my birth and childhood. Natchez, Mississippi is a beautiful town filled with majestic oak, pine, and Magnolia trees (the Magnolia blossom is the state flower).

The summertimes of my childhood brought a sweltering heat and suffocating humidity, slowing everything and everybody down. Three O'clock in the afternoon came cloaked in a sultry, sleepy stillness as young and old alike sought shelter from the humid haze, napping in the shade on the wrap-around front porches, or beneath the huge moss-draped oak trees that symbolized the old south. As Bobbie Gentry sang in her hit, "Ode To Billy Joe:" "It was the third of June, another sleepy dusty Delta day."

There was one creature, however, that never slept. The Mississippi Mosquito was a legendary nuisance - attempting to

2.

ruin every picnic, baseball game, and restful nap by its pesky presence. It was not unusual to be suddenly slapped in the face or arm by a friend or sibling, followed by a grin and a one word explanation: "Mosquito." One was never quite convinced of the validity of the claim until the rescuer pointed to the remains of the critter, evoking a mumbled "thanks" from the delivered.

The heat seemed to fuel the mosquitoes feeding frenzy, and one-bug-at-a-time pest control could never turn the tide in the favor of us human beings (or as my seven year-old brain heard: "Human Beans!") There had to be a better way to claim our rightful dominion over these winged nuisances.

There was: *The Fog-a-Machine!*

Many a summer's reverie was interrupted by the growing roar of the pesticide truck engine sounding its alarm. Help was on the way! It was time to wage chemical warfare against those pesky mosquitoes! The lazier ones among us were rousted, and a palpable excitement manifested itself in a shout: "Here comes the Fog-a Machine!" (Lest the reader think that we were easily entertained - which we usually were, but that's beside the point - by merely observing the puttering of an old truck spraying fog out of its hinder parts, read on!)

I still chuckle and shake my head in wonder as I recall running with my friends behind the pesticide truck that regularly patrolled the neighborhoods, leaving a cloud of dangerous chemicals in its wake. We tried to hold our breath and not get lost in the poisonous fog, giggling and calling out each other's names to make sure our comrades were safe.

Our parents warned us about following the fog truck, not so much because of the health dangers of breathing the stuff, but more out of a concern that we would lose our way and wander into the path of traffic. After three or four blocks of that euphoric entertainment, the five or six of us neighbor kids would give up the fight and roll together on the nearest lawn, laughing and holding our sides, gasping for breath. Who needed video games and computers?! Ah, the joys of childhood…

Most men worked at the Armstrong Tire and Rubber Company, International Paper, or in the booming oil industry. Like many southern towns, there was a peaceful co-existence between the "haves" and the "have-nots," at least on the surface. It didn't seem incongruous to me to see very nice houses on one block and dilapidated shacks on the next; that was just how things were in my home town.

The population of Adams County was about 25,000 when I was growing up. Some families lived in the beautiful antebellum mansions, opulent and elegant structures that evoked memories of the glory years in the mid 1800's, when Natchez had more millionaires per capita than any other city in the nation.

Every spring, people from all over the country and even the world would come to tour the homes during "Pilgrimage." We used to marvel at the many different license plates on the out-of-town vehicles.

Almost all of the tourists parked first at Stanton Hall, the stately mansion that served as the tour headquarters for the antebellum homes. As the visitors were greeted by volunteers in period costumes, including "Gone With The Wind" style hoop skirts, the well-to-do homeowners who had prepared all year for Pilgrimage proudly basked in the amazement and awe that their beautiful homes evoked from the appreciative tourists.

Most of the townspeople, however, lived as my family did, in the humbler abodes of the working class.

Natchez seemed to me to have more than its share of characters, secrets and stories. So did the Louis Baroni family.

4.

Roots

My grandparents on my father's side were from Genoa, Italy and moved to America early in the 1900's. In 1921 my father, Louis John Baroni was born in the growing Italian community in Natchez called "Little Italy."

He was next to the youngest of 14 children. Most of his older siblings had been born in Italy. My mother, Marjorie Rushing Baroni, had a Scottish-English heritage though her parents were both born in Mississippi.

My mom was raised Southern Baptist, as was most of the population, at least according to church membership roles. An old adage about the religious affiliation of folks in the South was that there were more Baptists than people! (Sometimes deceased members' names were "accidentally" kept on the membership rolls; of course, the Baptists didn't have a patent on this practice!)

Mama was the first of five children born to H.P. and Clem (Nannie) Rushing. Three sisters and beloved son, Carlton, followed my mother through the womb into life in Mississippi.

My Dad was a devout Roman Catholic, as were most of the Italians that found hope for a new life in Natchez. They brought the old ways from the Old Country and settled in, along with the substantial population of Irish Catholics, to membership in St. Mary's Parish. Most of the Italians lived, as my father's family did, in a close-knit community known as "Little Italy."

My dad quit school after the eighth grade to work in the fields with his sharecropper father. Both my parents were from sharecropper families; folks who worked the fields for the landowners were in return given shares of the bounty to feed their children and themselves. With a good harvest they were also given some of the crops to sell to scratch out a meager

5.

living. They didn't own their own land or homes but lived on the farm near the fields where they spent much of their lives.

There was not much thought given to higher education, or much time "wasted" dreaming of a better life for the children among most of the Italians. Just being in America was a dream come true and their lives, for the most part, were far better than the conditions of squalor and famine that had been Italy's lot in those days.

My father remembers the times as a young boy that he rode to the market on Saturdays in the horse-drawn wagon driven by his father Atilia. If business was good, Dad would receive a few cents to buy ice cream or a pickle. He didn't know for a long time that he was among the "poor." To him, family life was rich and life in his boyhood was an adventure.

He told me once about having a bit too much wine as a young teen during a neighborhood festive occasion. Normally shy, Dad jumped on a picnic table to boisterously belt out a song to the delight of the fellow revelers, and to the chagrin of the disciplinarian of the family, Noona, my grandmother!

My parents met at a high school football game. My mother played trumpet in the marching band for Natchez High. My handsome dad was "cattin' around" with some of his friends and snuck under the fence to avoid having to pay admission to the game, which was an important social event as well as an exciting athletic contest. Across the white chalk lines of a football field eyes met, hearts fluttered, and …. Ah, love in autumn!

Louis and Marge, so different in background, religion, and temperament, yet with a great deal in common, found each other and began to dream about life together.

After a whirlwind courtship they were married despite the vehement objections of my maternal grandmother, who in protest refused to attend the wedding. ("Marjorie Ray Rushing, that boy is a Catholic!") They were only 19 and 17 when they tied the knot. In time, to Nannie's further dismay, my mother converted to Catholicism.

Children soon followed their union. Their firstborn was Neil, then Mary Jane, Philip and Rose Ann. I came along in 1958. I was born at Natchez General Hospital and lived with my family in a small, comfortable house at 106 Oriole Terrace. Two years later, my brother Mark was born, completing the family portrait.

Southern (Musical) Exposure

Though I grew up in a small southern town, my parents and older brothers and sisters loved and listened to a wide variety of music. I was exposed to many different artists and styles. My mother listened to classical music, beloved gospel singer Mahalia Jackson, and even had Ray Charles' Country and Western album.

To this day, whenever I hear his version of "I Can't Stop Loving You," the plaintive, heartfelt music takes me back to the summer nights of my boyhood when I would sit on the porch and listen to Ray's soulful voice while I ate home-grown tomato sandwiches. It was sweet summertime and the living was easy.

Through my brother Neil, who was 16 years my senior and a jazz pianist, I was exposed to the eccentric sounds of Miles Davis, the funky Herbie Hancock, the haunting lyricism of pianist Bill Evans, and many other jazz musicians and singers. My other siblings introduced me to the magic of Motown and later the political activism of folk music and the raw energy of Rock and Roll.

Mississippi is the birth place of Elvis, the Delta Blues of B.B. King, and many other blues, rock, and gospel musicians. Legendary opera singer Leontyne Price was born here. Only 10 miles across the muddy Mississippi from Natchez, Jerry Lee Lewis and his cousins Jimmy Swaggart and Mickey Gilley grew up in tiny Ferriday, Louisiana.

My first musical epiphany happened at the home of a childhood friend Ronnie Bee. I was five or six years old and he introduced me to the first Beatles record I had ever heard. As I listened in awe to the harmonies, drums, and guitar sounds of "I Wanna Hold Your Hand," I was transfixed and transformed. It was, like my first kiss, almost more than my little heart could take. How could something sound so good? Other 45's followed: "Help," "A Hard Days Night," "Paperback Writer," "Yesterday," and my friend got them all!

I memorized and sang the "A" and "B" sides of every single the Beatles released. I know his mother must have gotten tired of me coming over. Thank you Ronnie Bee, wherever you are!

I started piano lessons at age five taught by Fred Stietenroth, a kind, gifted Jewish classical pianist. (Natchez had quite a diverse constituency for its size and location in the Deep South.) I took lessons for seven years, and though I must have learned how to read music a little bit, I basically tried to play by ear what my music teacher played. At the time I thought I was fooling him, but looking back I think Mr. Steitenroth just let me slide.

Maybe he recognized in me an unusual aptitude for music that we Mississippians call playing "by heart." That term is still an endearing one to me and sums up my musical philosophy: "If it don't make you feel, then it ain't really real." One of the first songs I learned by heart was Petula Clarke's version of the popular radio hit of that day, "Downtown."

My musical journey had begun.

The Civil Rights Days

One of the most profound experiences of my childhood happened because of my mother. My mama believed that "people were people." Skin color didn't matter, everyone was worthy of respect and dignity. With the unwavering support of my dad, she put her beliefs into action in the 1960's, in the south, *in Mississippi!*

Those were the torrid days of the KKK, segregation, lynching, cross burnings and fire hoses, boycotts and riots. My mother got very involved in the Civil Rights Movement, one of the few white women in the town (or the state for that matter) to do so.

Dad had to endure the stares and slurs of some of his co-workers at Armstrong Tire and Rubber Co. Some of the men he worked with day in and day out were fervent members of the K.K.K.

One of the black men that worked at the same factory lost both legs to a car bomb planted in his vehicle. My father remembers placing small pebbles on the hood of his car to help him determine whether or not his automobile had been tampered with.

Periodically the Klan would roll up one page newsletters filled with malicious gossip that we called "hate-sheets" and leave them in peoples' driveways. When I was a small boy, I would pick them up on occasion to find that my own family was the subject of the vilification. Fortunately, at age five or six, I was too young to comprehend much of what was going on.

Along with Mom and Dad, my older siblings, Mary Jane Philip and Rose Ann, bore much of the brunt of the ostracism and name calling. The threat of violence hovered like an ominous cloud over most small Mississippi towns in the early 1960's.

One night my sister Rose Ann was walking in our neighborhood with some of her friends. A car they had never seen before was driving back and forth down our street. After a few runs up and down, the driver pulled over and asked my sister if she knew where the Baroni's lived. My sister smartly misdirected him and ran home to tell my father.

What happened next has become a favorite part of our family history. My usually peaceful dad got his shotgun; (unloaded, but the guy didn't know that), and ran out to the strange car, pointed the shotgun at the ashen-faced driver and in no uncertain terms commanded him to get out of there and not come back. He rapidly complied and we never saw him again.

Go dad!

We Shall Overcome

It was in that environment that my mother began to take me to voter registration rallies. These were events held in small black churches. Much of the impetus of the Civil Rights Movement came out of the African-American church, which was a strong unifying and galvanizing force in the black community. The rallies were held to encourage black people to register to vote. Though by this time they had a legal right to vote, some black folks were subjected to intimidation and harassment if they tried to register.

Most of the time my mom and siblings and I were the only white people to attend these meetings. It was an almost surreal atmosphere. People would use funeral home fans to try to wave away the stifling summer heat.

As a young boy, I didn't understand most of what was going on. I can't remember the speeches and other items on the agenda, but there was one thing about those meetings I will never forget: the singing.

Between speeches the choir would sing. It was usually a small choir, from 20 to 30 voices. There was no P.A. system, no microphones. They did not need amplification! As passionate voices were raised singing "We Shall Overcome" and "Ain't Gonna Let Nobody Turn Me 'Round," the congregation and choir alike would weep, sing, shout and celebrate like nothing this young white child had ever seen, heard or *felt*!

I didn't realize it then, but God gave me gifts in those sweltering churches. I experienced the passion in music, songs delivered with emotion and honesty. I heard music employed to serve a cause greater than merely to draw praise to the singer or entertain the crowd. I received the ability to appreciate people's differences and celebrate the many things we have in common.

Those wonderful people gave me the bequest of faith-filled songs that transcend suffering and give hope in the midst of struggle and despair. I didn't realize it at the time but seeds of destiny were planted in my heart, and many gifts were poured like living water into this young man on those hot, humid, Natchez nights.

-2-
Adolescent Adventures

America had just stumbled through the turbulent sixties. The Beatles latest release was the White Album. I flattered myself that I did a pretty Good imitation of Paul McCartney singing "Rocky Raccoon." I also sang along to Diana Ross and the Supremes. Before my voice changed I did a fair Diana Ross impression!

There was a local band called "My Generation" that practiced in a storefront building across from the Malt Shop, a popular local hangout. These guys had electric guitars, big Marshall amps, drums *and* congas, a bass guitar and a Hammond B-3 organ. They had their own P.A. system, overcoming a major obstacle that kept many garage bands languishing in obscurity.

They also had groupies. To this 12 year-old musical wannabe they were big time! "My Generation" played a few original tunes, and cover versions of Three Dog Night, Steppenwolf and other rock bands of the day. They sounded "just like the record," the litmus test of excellence to the ears of me and my music-loving friends.

One of my friends was a 14 year old wunderkind guitar player named Pat Hornsby. He was starting a band and they wanted me to be the lead singer! We began to practice in an upper bedroom of our house on the hill at 503 Monroe St. (We had moved across town from Oriole Terrace a few years earlier). Considering how loudly we played, it's a wonder the cops only showed up a couple of times to tell us to turn it down.

This was before the age of portable keyboards, we couldn't mic a piano loudly enough and couldn't afford a Hammond B-3 organ, so I just sang.

The name of this first band was "Cannabis Sativa," the Latin name for marijuana! Pat and I wrote our own three chord theme song with the same title. Even though later I began smoking pot; this song was actually an anti-drug song. Of course the guitars and drums were so loud no one could hear the words anyway!

I remember our first paying gig at the youth Canteen Dance. We made $100 and split it four ways. Wow! Money for playing music! I thought I was in heaven!

A year of performing with just two guitars, drums and singer without a bass player gave me a desire to learn how to play bass guitar. My parents helped me buy an Epiphone beginner's bass and soon I was holed up in my room with the stereo, playing along with "Smoke On The Water" (Deep Purple), Led Zeppelin, Black Sabbath and the somewhat softer folk-rock sounds of Crosby, Stills, Nash and Young. I also gleefully jammed along with the latest recordings from Stevie Wonder, and of course, all the other Motown music.

My brother Neil also graciously played jazz piano while I plunked along on the bass. He taught me basic music theory as well.

I wrote a few hormonally inspired love songs and used a technique called "multi-tracking" to record some of them. I would play piano and sing lead into a reel-to-reel tape recorder. Then I would play that tape back and play bass and sing harmony into a Radio Shack cassette recorder along with it. The end result was mostly room noise and tape hiss but I learned some things that I still use in recording today. It was so much fun!

Troubled Waters

I was growing musically and athletically. Like my brothers and sisters, I excelled in basketball and baseball. I also developed a love for reading and an appreciation for words that I have to this day.

However, socially, I felt inept and estranged from those around me. I felt that I was different and didn't fit in. An awkward self-consciousness began to paralyze me.

There were some obvious reasons.

Our family's civil rights work caused all of us to be subjected to a certain amount of rejection and ostracism. My sisters' friends couldn't spend the night with them for fear that our house would be bombed in the night. I was called a "nigger lover" on more than one occasion. Once, when I was about six years old, a neighborhood bully called me that and threatened to beat me up, but I ran. I told my family about the near-miss and they applauded my evasive maneuvers. (The boy was older and stronger.)

By this time my mother was the personal secretary for the mayor of Fayette, Ms., twenty-two miles away in rural

14.

Jefferson County. Charles Evers was the first elected black mayor in Mississippi since just after the Civil War. His brother Medgar, a hero and martyr of the civil rights movement, had been shot-gunned to death outside of his Jackson home in 1963.

The racial battle lines had been drawn and we had made our choice to be a part of the equality movement. I was proud of my mother and our family's stance and believed in "the cause," yet I couldn't help wishing that I fit in a little better in social situations and at my school, the parochial St. Mary's Cathedral.

There were also darker reasons for my loneliness and the sense that I was on the outside looking in at life. Earlier in my childhood I had been sexually abused. I was only seven or eight years old at the time. The perpetrator was a neighbor boy and the abuse caused me to feel very confused about my identity and sexuality; though of course I didn't understand any of that at the time. Later abuse by others compounded my feelings of worthlessness and fear of rejection.

In my troubled teen years, music became the source of my security, identity and escape from my inner turmoil. Music was the tangible fantasy where I tried to hide from the ugliness of the world and the ugliness I felt within me. Every time I would hear a favorite recording, the song was always the same.

Music was safe, emotionally satisfying, predictable and dependable.

Real life was not like that for me. In addition to my insecurity and sense of displacement, my mother seemed to vent her frustrations and the pressures of the changing racial climate on her family. Often she would erupt in rage if things didn't go her way, perhaps I was overly sensitive to her at times, but I use to cringe and feel paralyzed when she would raise her voice, no matter who the target of her anger happened to be.

When I went to parties, I would stay by the wall, a real "wallflower," until someone noticed me there and invited me to play the piano.

Though I pretended indifference and tried to play it cool, inwardly I was relieved to sit behind the piano keyboard because I felt safe and loved there.

Besides music and books, my other safe places were the basketball court and the baseball field. I loved sports, especially basketball.

This was in the day when basketball legend "Pistol" Pete Maravich starred at Louisiana State University. He changed the game with his fancy behind-the-back passing and mesmerizing ball-handling skills. His collegiate career scoring average of over 40 points a game (*before* the three-point shot was instituted!) still stands today and may never be surpassed.

Pete had long hair, wore floppy white socks (that he never washed) under his purple and gold ones, and was my hero. Maravich was the only acceptable reason that Mississippi boys could cheer for hated LSU, an arch-rival of Ole Miss. Thank God that during football season we could cheer for Ole Miss, largely because of their legendary scrambling quarterback, Archie Manning, a grid-iron icon who later played for the New Orleans Saints in the NFL and raised two star quarterback sons, Peyton and Eli.

I emulated Pete Maravich on the basketball court, wearing floppy socks, long hair, and an LSU purple and gold wristband that clashed horribly with our green and white uniforms. Just as I had in music, I approached basketball in a non-traditional way.

16.

I developed a fancy, crowd pleasing way to pass, shoot and dribble that endeared me to most fans and gave Coach Mike Durr headaches. I threw behind the back passes (that sometimes caught even my teammates by surprise) and dribbled behind my back and between my legs.

I really didn't do it primarily to show off- though I admit I relished the attention- I just had a love for the sport and since I was shorter than most of the other players, I used my ball handling, quick thinking and passing skills to make up for my height disadvantage.

Once, in a district tournament game, with our team one point behind and only a few seconds left in the last quarter, I dribbled down-court and put the ball through my opponent's legs. Then I raced behind him, catching my own pass and scoring a lay up at the buzzer that won the game! The Pistol would have been proud.

Years later I met Pete at a men's retreat in North Carolina. He listened to a concert I performed and I got to tell him of his influence in my life.

When I wasn't playing or practicing sports or music, I enjoyed hanging around with my friends, mostly guys from our neighborhood.

Sometimes we would get into trouble, breaking into peoples homes, "egging" cars, shooting bottle rockets at passing vehicles or, as we got older, driving way too fast. I don't think we were bad kids, just not given enough positive direction by our parents and older kids that perhaps could have better influenced our lives. We had a sense of immortality that most teen-agers have.

I hung around with 5 or 6 boys that went to the same school. We made up our own games and the fun that we had sometimes got reckless. We chose teams and had wars using

17.

fireworks. One time I shot a bottle-rocket (somewhat accidentally) that landed in my younger brother Mark's jacket pocket. Unfortunately the pocket was filled with fireworks that exploded out if his pocket. Oops! (Thankfully he was unhurt; I can't say the same for the jacket.)

My friends Ridge Partridge and Scott Ramagos built a small bomb from a chemistry set. It exploded prematurely, sending Ridge to the hospital for skin grafts over his badly burned thighs. It could have been worse. Again, we weren't really bad kids; we were just not very smart sometimes.

I was spared from death several times that I knew about and probably many other times of which I was blissfully unaware.

One night my brother Mark and I went "joyriding" in my friend's father's mint condition Mustang. He asked where we could go to find out what kind of speed the car had. I had heard some older kids talk about the impromptu drag races on Cargill Road, so I told my friend that that would be a good place to go speeding in the Mustang.

What we didn't realize was that there was a certain straight stretch of the road that was safer for racing. We had had a few beers and were ready for some excitement.

Unfortunately, we started speeding on Cargill Road well before the straightaway and my friend David lost control of that beautiful Mustang, hitting the brakes at 70 miles-an-hour around a curve *crossing the railroad tracks!*

Everything spun around and we rolled over into a ditch and turned back upright. Miraculously, none of us was seriously hurt (except the Mustang, which was a total loss).

After walking and finding a phone and calling my friend's father (gulp), Mark and I were dropped off at our home.

We were so traumatized that we walked straight to the kitchen and started washing dishes! That should have been a dead giveaway to our parents that something momentous had happened. Teen-age boys in my day didn't wash dishes until they had been asked at least three times!

When we saw the remains of that car the next afternoon, I knew that God had spared our lives.

Though I was the leading scorer and MVP of our basketball team, made good grades, popular in school and with the young ladies, and seemed to have almost everything going my way, I was not comfortable in my own skin. I didn't know who I really was. Often I walked around Natchez by myself at night and cried. My loneliness was much deeper than girlfriend problems and the dreaded pimples on my face, I just didn't realize it then.

Evolution Revolution

I can still hear the crowd of 10,000 strong in the Mississippi Coliseum shouting in surprise and joy: "Sing it! - Come on with it white boy!" "That's awRIGHT!"

Our band, "Evolution Revolution" (we thought it was a cool name back then) was playing at the annual Medgar Evers Memorial Homecoming in Jackson, about two hours from Natchez.

It was 1973. I was the fifteen year old bass player and the only white person in the group. I mostly just played and accompanied the fine organist and singer Tony Gordon, and the drummer, little Joe Frazier.

Joe's little sister Daneese and her friend were our 11 year old "dancing girls.' They were good too! I sang one or two songs in our repertoire including the Dobie Gray hit "Drift Away."

The crowd that day was warm and encouraging to our young group. Then it was my turn to sing. I started the song… "Day after day I'm more confused…" The response was deafening! The people shouted and "high-fived" each other and made me feel at home. I don't know if it was the novelty of a young white kid with a bit of soul in his voice, or if they were just being kind, but to this day I love the responsiveness of many African-American people to my singing and playing. They help me "preach" the song.

To top off that extraordinary day, that evening I got to meet the legendary B.B. King. Nobody can make heartache and tough times feel so good like the blues master and his guitar companion, "Lucille!"

Us white folks owe a debt of gratitude to African Americans because we are beneficiaries of the gifts of celebration, emotional expression and honest passion that God has given to people of color. Out of the rock of struggle comes the sweetness of the honey of God's grace to the downtrodden.

Our band didn't stay together long, but we parted as friends and though we went our separate ways, together we share some treasured memories. After 30 years of virtually no communication, just recently I received an email from Daneese.

Now happily married with children, she found my web-site and wrote to say hello and to inform me that she is glad to see what I am doing with my music, and that she is leading the dance team at her church!

Some circles stay unbroken.

-3-
Fancy Music

From the time that I first learned to read, I have been a lover of words. Our house on Monroe Street was filled with books: books crammed into the floor-to-ceiling shelves in the main hallway, books stacked in various bedrooms, books in closets. Words by the billions filled the home.

My mother instilled that love of reading in me. One image from her hardscrabble childhood is that of my mother Marge laying in the summer shade on her back with yet another book opened before her, while the rest of the family went about their chores. Young Marge was so into her dream world of words and adventures in print that when her mother asked her to take the family horse to the barn; she didn't even know which of the horses on the farm they sharecropped on was theirs! That would be like a child today not knowing which car in the driveway belonged to the family.

Books were an escape from the hard reality that was her life. She had an abusive alcoholic father and a strong-willed mother who was hard-pressed to teach some common sense to her daughter the daydreamer.

My family was open to a lot of influences politically and spiritually, some were noble, some experimental, and some outrageous!

This was reflected on our bookshelves. Books by Catholic mystics like Thomas Merton and St. Francis of Assisi shared space with pioneer psychologist Carl Jung and the heavy writings of Tolstoy and Dostoevsky (literally heavy as well; they were big, thick books). Then there were the fun books: Agatha Christie murder mysteries and my favorite Hardy Boys and Nancy Drew detective adventures.

I remember walking to the Natchez public library regularly as an eager young boy and filling my library card quota for the week with science fiction books by Robert Heinlein, Ray Bradbury, C.S. Lewis, and others. These fantasies about outer space inspired my fledgling attempts at songwriting. One of the first songs I ever wrote (and mercifully have forgotten) was about a visit to planet "X."

We also had a lot of books about mental illness. My oldest brother Neil, the jazz musician, wrestled with severe depression and chemical imbalance and had a life-long struggle with it. Though he could play music that moved people to tears by its beauty, he endured the loss of his marriage and did not see his two sons for almost thirty years. (In his later years they were reunited and Neil cultivated a relationship with his sons and grandchildren.)

Throughout his life, he maintained the Baroni wit, a wry, light-hearted, insulating, cynicism that was passed down from grandmother Nannie, who was as sweet and funny as she was ornery. My father is the king of corny jokes, but according to my children I am close to inheriting his throne!

Humor, books, sports and music - that in a nutshell explains how I coped with my sensitive, artistic, creative personality, the fear of our family being attacked because of our civil rights involvement, and the trauma of the sexual abuse and intense family dynamics of those formative years.

I also had girlfriends. They were many; they were wonderful (well, most of them). Sadly I didn't have a clue as to what a healthy friendship, much less relationship, looked like. If any of you are reading this, I ask for your forgiveness for my selfishness, and for me being such a jerk.

"High"er Education

My junior and senior years of high school were spent in a blur of playing basketball and music, going to parties and drinking beer and smoking dope. I managed to function pretty well most of the time, maintaining my grades and keeping up appearances for my preoccupied parents.

After my illustrious senior basketball season (the mighty Green Wave went 4-20 though I must add that most of the teams we played were from much larger schools), I went to college at the University of Southern Mississippi in Hattiesburg.

Though my declared major was jazz music, my chief interest was smoking dope. I remember groaning at the thought of having to wake up "so early" to go to an 11:40 A.M. first class! Needless to say, I was undisciplined and unfocused. I did keep practicing the bass guitar (my main instrument at the time), and though I didn't read music, my ear was good enough that every now and then I got to sit in with the Jazz Lab Band conducted by Raoul Jerome.

I called my parents with three weeks to go in that first year, wanting to come home. By this time I knew that I wanted to *play* music rather than teach, and a jazz degree wouldn't give me the experience and education that actually playing music professionally could. They convinced me to stay and at least finish one year of college.

Those were the last three weeks of my formal education.

Boys in the Band

While at USM, I became friends with Stuart Redd, the guitar player from a band called "Fancy Music." They had played at nicer show clubs in Detroit, New Orleans, Pennsylvania, and other parts of the country. Stuart, from nearby Laurel, Mississippi, was attending USM because the group's lead singer developed vocal nodules and required one year of complete vocal rest. Redd, an affable guy, told me after my college year was over that the band was starting up again and needed a keyboard player. This was the Disco 70's and most bands needed keyboardists.

I put my fretless bass back in its case for a while and boarded a bus to Detroit to join the band. At the ripe old age of 18 I began my professional musical career in earnest.

My first gig with Tom Elias and Fancy Music was at the Stowaway Lounge in the Flying Dutchman Motel in Warren, Michigan, a Detroit suburb. Though this indeed was the age of disco, we were NOT a disco band.

During our shows, we donned long-tailed Tuxedos and top hats and canes and did pop/rock/jazz arrangements of music from the 1910's, and 20's. We performed Al Jolson songs complete with Tom made up in "white face" instead of Jolson's blackface routine. We also did our own arrangements of music from Broadway shows including "Cabaret," "Chicago," and "The Wiz."

In the Broadway remake of "The Wizard of OZ," Tom sang a song called "Home"… "When I think of home, I think of a place where there's love overflowing..." Just thinking about that song almost brings me to tears. Our audience generally responded to our group with warm (though sometimes slightly drunken) enthusiasm.

24.

As much as I enjoyed the novelty of playing the shows, I enjoyed the dance sets more. As Tom rested between shows (in which his dancing, singing, acting and passion caused him to expend enormous amounts of energy, no matter the size of the crowd), the band would play Earth, Wind, and Fire, Stevie Wonder, Boz Scaggs, and even some of our own music.

Sometimes we would get into extended solos and jazz that stoked the musical fires in me. I also enjoyed singing in the group. I did some solos and back-up vocals.

For almost two years I traveled the country with Fancy Music playing a Yamaha Electric Grand piano and an Elka string ensemble. I had no debts, and made a comfortable salary for a single guy. Unwisely, I blew most of it on pot and a few other drugs.

Gene Houston, our drummer (who later played with Pam Tillis and other country and rock stars), taught me a lot about musical discipline, timing, and fitting in musically with the rest of the group. Until then I was basically a show-off, just like on the basketball court in high school, doing my own thing. I thought I was displaying my skills, instead I was merely highlighting my musical (and personal) immaturity. Just because one *can* improvise, it doesn't mean that one should.

There was a sense of community in the band that I appreciated. Even with our whirlwind travel schedule and dreams of stardom we genuinely liked each other.

Some of the rehearsals got tense, but the tension didn't last long. One of the crazier things we did was to get stoned together and listen to Frederick K. Price teaching tapes! Rev. Price was a "Word of Faith" preacher from Crenshaw Center in Los Angeles that the light man, Cubby McDonald, introduced us to. (Maybe some of that good Word got planted in my heart!)

25.

Even though I had a dream gig, when I would get still and sober enough, I realized that there was a growing restlessness and emptiness in me that music, philosophy, going to church, girlfriends, and dope couldn't satisfy.

-4-
<u>How High's the Water Mama?</u>

There is a photograph in our family collection that made the wall of honor in the dining room. It is a picture of me at 14 years of age sitting on the bluff overlooking the muddy Mississippi. I had long hair and was playing my guitar with my back to the camera. I didn't know I was being photographed.

That shot by a local newspaper photographer was published on the front page of the Natchez Democrat, one of Mississippi's oldest daily papers. The caption asked: "How High's the Water, Mama?" That was the title of a popular country song of the day. It was a very good question. I could easily imagine an answer from my intense, fearful, courageous mother: " The water is very high, flood stage, deep and dark and wide."

It is hard to overestimate the influence that a mother has on a child, especially a son. To think about Mama and our relationship provokes in me strong, ambivalent feelings.

After years of denial, introspection, counseling, and just plain living life, two fundamental, powerful and conflicting messages from my mother wrestle inside me like Jacob and Esau to this day. In the depths of my soul Mama taught me that I was "Special" and "Selfish."

At first glance, it would appear that the first word is positive and the second is overwhelmingly negative. Therefore the obvious solution to my emotional struggle seems to be that I should just accept the first verdict; that I am unique, gifted, "special," and simply discard the second as the ranting of an overbearing parent who was under a lot of pressure from without and within. If my internal landscape was that easy to navigate, I could have saved a great deal of money spent on professional help over the years!

The fact is, she was right *and* wrong on both counts. It has taken me a lot of hard work to begin to reconcile that. In fact, though I am light-years from where I started, in some ways I am still on the quest to find out, and to love and accept, who I really am.

Marge Baroni was an idealist, a dreamer and a fighter. She would not hesitate to get on the phone and call the mayor, the governor, or even the President of the United States if she thought it would help to correct an injustice.

She tearfully pled my case to the elementary school principal so that I would be allowed to enroll in the overcrowded third grade at Cathedral Elementary (my parents wanted me to have a Catholic education).

A Change Gonna Come

"Margie" (as she despised being called by her condescending "friends"), couldn't abide the status quo that so many in the south seemed comfortable to just accept. She had learned some of that from her mother, who refused to allow her children to call black people "nigger." This was in a time when that epithet was almost universally used by white folks in Mississippi. My grandmother Nannie, a tough minded yet compassionate nurse who grew up in Brookhaven, Miss., taught her young daughter to respect people regardless of their skin color or station in life.

Mama loved us as best she could, and, like most parents, hoped that her children would achieve far more than she did. She insisted that all her children start music lessons and that the girls take ballet classes, even though those things cost money and were deemed unnecessary extravagances by most of the working class. I suspect my dad thought so too sometimes, but in this case Mama's arguments prevailed.

My mother was proud of my musical aptitude. She loved it when I would play piano for her friends or in public settings and encouraged me often to do that. In retrospect, I wonder if she felt that it was not just my ability, but her motherhood that was also on display. As courageous as she was, and as stubborn and impervious to criticism that she seemed to be most of the time, my mom, like most people, yearned for the approval and acceptance of others.

Whatever her motivation, I quickly learned to feel at home in the spotlight. I still love the sound of applause. Through my childhood and teen-age years I learned that I was loved unconditionally… especially when I performed. I was "special."

Mom also branded me "selfish." I think her motivation to do so was a deadly combination of the results of her growing up in a scary, alcoholic home, the dreams and ambitions she felt obligated to repress because she became a wife and a mother at the tender age of 18, and the extraordinarily fearful times of the '60's.

Also she had some good old-fashioned guilt (Baptist *and* Catholic - guilt is non-denominational), a genuine desire to make a difference in the world, and a Messiah/martyr complex thrown in that caused Mama to project her aspirations upon the rest of us.

Many times she called me selfish. Sometimes she was right. I've already admitted that I sometimes cared more about my peers' acceptance than our family's civil-rights stance. However, instead of my mother understanding that mine was the natural response of a teenager looking to fit in, and at least acknowledging that she knew where I was coming from, I felt that she shamed me for not having an adult's viewpoint, though I was just a kid.

This seeming disdain for my point of view was just one of the many times that I was the target of what I have come to realize was her own frustration with the world and herself.

Of course I still have childish, self-absorbed moments, but now I know that being self-caring is not the same thing as being selfish.

It has also been healing for me to realize that in one sense I am not special (though I'm delightful most of the time, of course). How freeing to be wonderfully ordinary. I am a human being; I am merely and extraordinarily a man!

Though I do want to make a difference in my world, and I dare to believe that I can, I've resigned my position as "Messiah-in-Training." Besides, that job has already been filled by Someone most qualified.

I've inherited quite a legacy from my mother, who died of cancer at the age of 63 in March of 1986. I am grateful to have known her and glad that she has finally found the peace, justice, and freedom she fought so valiantly and desperately for her whole life. Her voice is not as strong in my heart and mind as it used to be... and that is how it should be.

At her funeral at St. Mary's Basilica in Natchez, with a multi-colored, trans-generational and eclectic crowd gathered to remember her and mourn her passing, I sang a song I had written. It was inspired by what became Dr. Martin Luther King's last speech:

I've been to the mountaintop and seen the sky
I'm going to my homeland there, bye and bye
So don't go mourning for me when I die,
'Cause I've been to the mountaintop and seen the sky!

So, now I can respond with my own answer to the question. How high's the water, Mama? It's deep and high, dark and wide, but I've learned, just as you have, that it's crossable. Mama, it's crossable now.

-5-
<u>New Orleans and Beyond</u>

Fancy Music played together for the last time with me as keyboard player in the spring of 1978. Our last engagement was in New Orleans at the mouth of the French Quarter: Top of the Marriot. It was time for me to move on. The only problem was that I didn't know where to go next. Thankfully, I had a refuge at my parent's home in Natchez. (It's such a weird feeling to leave home to go to college then move back in to find that home is not quite my home anymore.)

I rested, caught up with some old friends, rested some more, played a bit of music, listened to a lot of music. Still using vinyl records, I almost wore out recordings by Steely Dan, Weather Report (with prodigy fretless bass player Jaco Pastorius), the Pat Metheny Group, the Lee Ritenour "Captain Fingers" album, Joni Mitchell, and good ole James Taylor.

Sitting with the headphones on, listening to a stack of 6 LP's at a time, reminded me of my job as a cashier at a local self-service gas station. I was sixteen and worked the graveyard shift the summer after my junior year of high school.

This shift was an experiment for the owners that eventually didn't work; after all, Natchez was a very small town. After midnight I usually would only have 5 or 6 customers until sunrise, so I would sit in my little booth and listen to music all night! Whether it was the lateness of the hour, the solitude of the job, or the emotional content of the music (probably all of the above); I will always treasure that time.

Here I was, back in Natchez again with no job and no prospects, like a paddle-wheel steamboat set adrift. As weeks went by, I gained weight and lost track of time. It's funny how too much rest can lead to restlessness. I needed something to do, I needed a plan. I called my brother Neil in New Orleans.

1514 Euterpe St.

The trolley was once a main mode of transportation in New Orleans (it's still in use today). The main trolley line ran from the heart of the French Quarter with its burlesque joints, jazz clubs, and fine restaurants, to the outlying areas of downtown. The end of one trolley line was St. Charles Ave., with its wonderful French architecture, immaculate lawns, and beautiful, spacious homes. Unfortunately, Neil didn't live in one of those. I went to live with him in a small, though comfortable, apartment just off St. Charles - at 1514 Euterpe Street.

We could almost smell the beignets (French doughnuts) and the Cajun coffee brewing in the deli just around the corner. Neil and I had many a delicious muffaleta (a round deli sandwich big enough for two), and New Orleans style pizza in those hazy, lazy days.

By this time Neil had been divorced for quite a few years, and was attempting to make a living playing piano at the hotels and clubs in the Big Easy. It wasn't so easy for him as he battled with severe depression, grieved not seeing or talking to his sons, and tried to give his floundering younger brother some sense of direction.

One mild fall afternoon, we went to a neighborhood park. I remember sitting in the grass staring up at the clouds and feeling such a sense of lost-ness. Neil tried to help but he didn't really know what to say. Though I appreciated his efforts, it was very much a case of the blind leading the blind.

I do have some fond memories (besides the food) of those times. We would jam in the apartment, sometimes inviting guests to participate. One time a virtuoso guitarist named Emily Remler came to play at our house. A fantastic guitar player, I mostly watched with mouth agape as she showed her mastery of the instrument. I was saddened to hear a few years later on PBS radio that she passed away at a young age. The world should have heard more of her music.

Though I didn't have a steady gig, I did play with Neil on a few occasions, thumping my bass and watching the people as they mostly ignored us and partied. To this day, I am sensitive about whether or not people listen to the music.

We got the most enthusiastic response from fellow musicians. Their encouragement and our love for the music itself was enough to keep us going.

I loved going to other musicians' houses in New Orleans and having extended jam sessions. Usually we played with a combo: Neil on keyboard, I played bass, a drummer (I heard some amazing drummers), a sax player, and possibly a guitar player. It was music for the sheer joy of it, music for music's sake and it was glorious! There is something amazing and intangible that sometimes happens when a group of players begin to play spontaneously, intuitively following each other on what at times is an exhilarating adventure in sound.

The drummer lays down a groove, sometimes we start with a familiar tune like Herbie Hancock's haunting "Maiden Voyage" (I love the titles of some of those jazz tunes). Then, with a nod, it's the sax players turn to improvise or "solo," then the keyboard, then the bass.

The music ebbs and flows like a supernatural tide, sometimes we ride the waves, sometimes the waves wash over us and the song is alive, moving, breathing through our fingers and our hearts. When we felt really wild and crazy we would just start out with a new spontaneous composition. Sometimes there were musical "train wrecks," but when the flow was there we all knew it and we loved it. Neil taught me that if you played a wrong note, just repeat it and folks will think you did it on purpose.

I am told that the six-piece rock group "Grateful Dead" sometimes had these experiences in concert where all the players spontaneously played a new, unrehearsed, *unwritten* song as one man, instinctively playing together. A member of the group said that when that happened, they knew that the "Seventh Man" had arrived.

I am grateful for the spirit of musical adventure that I learned to cultivate largely from those New Orleans jazz musicians.

The weirdest job I ever had was playing bass in the French Quarter during Mardi Gras - the city-wide excuse to party and go wild - that happens every year right before Lent.

My shift started at midnight and ended at 5:00 A.M. I will never forget seeing one of the patrons, obviously under the influence of some strange kind of mind-altering drug, walk around with what looked like pinwheels in her eyes. Though by that time I had done a few pretty strange drugs myself, the lost look on that woman's face freaked me out. I was glad to leave the club and greet the sunrise after that night.

"We're Going To Jackson"

Then I got the phone call that moved me closer toward to the rendezvous with my musical and spiritual destiny. Once again it was a guitar player. (What is it with these guitar players? First Pat Hornsby, my childhood friend, then Kevin Dukes, my room-mate from college who went on to play with top artists like Jackson Browne, then Stuart Redd from Fancy Music, and now Jimmy English, from Laurel, Mississippi, who had replaced Stuart in that group.)

Jimmy called to say that a group of musicians were thinking about moving to Jackson, Miss. to work in a recording studio: North American Recording Company (wryly called "Narc" by all of us musician types). He told me that they needed an extra keyboard player-vocalist. I wasn't exactly taking the New Orleans music scene by storm with my bass playing, though thankfully Neil didn't let me starve.

When Jimmy told me about an amazing and beautiful singer-songwriter named Kim Morrisson from Nashville, a studio singer with a six octave range who made people cry with the poignancy of her songs, I was convinced. Good-bye N'awlins, hello Jackson!

Slick at C.W. Goodnight's!

I moved to Jackson in the middle of the great flood of 1978. The water had overflowed the banks of the Ross Barnett Reservoir and flooded auto dealerships, homes, and even the Mississippi Coliseum where I had sung as a teenager.

After the rain-swollen streets and levees around the reservoir dried up, so did most of the studio work. Our group consisted of drummer Owen Hale (who later played with Lynrd Skynrd and many other bands and artists), guitarist Jimmy English, bassist Ralph Smith, synthesizer virtuoso Chalmers Davis, I sang and played electric piano, and fronting the band was the lovely and talented Kim Morrisson.

Needing to work, we grudgingly took our rather substantial musical abilities to the disco on the reservoir.

We had a stupid name and played stupid songs in a stupid club that also had a stupid name (I'm not bitter about that period of my life or anything)!

We called ourselves Kim Morrisson and "Slick," the club was "C.W. Goodnight's," and if I never hear "I Will Survive" again, it will be too soon!

Our lead vocalist Kim was a brilliant songwriter. In a subtle rebellion against the mindless disco invasion that threatened to take over the music world, she only learned 2 of the song's bazillion or so verses, singing them over and over. The bouncing, drunken patrons either didn't notice or didn't mind!

My dreams of playing meaningful music to an enlightened, appreciative audience had run aground on the shallow disco shores of the Ross Barnett Reservoir.

36.

Some of the only oases in my musical desert came when I got to play and sing some Bill Withers ("Ain't No Sunshine When She's Gone," "Lean On Me"), Boz Scaggs ("Lowdown"), and Billy Joel songs ("My Life," "I Love You Just the Way You Are"). Though I hesitate to admit it, in the interest of full self-disclosure I must confess that I also liked the infectious beat of "Play That Funky Music White Boy."

Internally, my sense of displacement and restlessness only increased, but like New Orleans, my time in Jackson would be short-lived.

-6-
<u>Fame</u>

The man wore jeans, expensive leather boots, a fancy cowboy hat, and a boyish smirk as he ambled through the heavy door into the control room in Recording Studio A. He deliberately placed a bottle of Jim Beam whiskey next to the sound console. With all eyes on him, he dramatically retrieved a pistol from his pocket, placed it by the whiskey bottle, sat down and pressed the "talkback" button. This enabled him to be heard in the isolation booths by the veteran session musicians that largely depended on this man and his production prowess for their livelihood. He smiled and winked at the sound engineer then drawled, "All right now boys, let's cut some hits."

This is one of the legends told about the visionary studio owner and pioneer Rick Hall of Muscle Shoals, Alabama. It is no small indication of his aspirations and confidence that he named the studio "Fame Recording Studios" before anyone had ever heard of it or him.

Who would have dreamed that in a relatively short amount of time recording artists as popular and diverse as Aretha Franklin, Paul Anka, Percy Sledge ("When a Man Loves A Woman"), The Osmond Brothers (including their first hit

"One Bad Apple" - a Jackson Five sound-alike), and one of my vocal heroes, Dobie Gray ("Drift Away", "Lovin' Arms"), along with many other country, rock and pop stars would all record in the hit factory that became Fame Studios. The sign still adorns the original studio building:

"Fame: Where It All Started."

Rick Hall's success was due to several factors. He was a shrewd businessman, a good judge of talent, and he had an ear for mining hit songs.

Probably the smartest thing he did was surround himself with musicians whose skill, and diversity was legendary: the "Fame Gang."

These guys could play almost any style and make it ring true. They had the musical ability to make you *feel* what they played. The sound of these players and singers (still some of the best female background vocalists anywhere) became known as "The Muscle Shoals Sound."

Although Muscle Shoals was only about two and a half hours from Nashville, there was a distinction in the music that could be heard and felt.

One reason was that Rick was the first major studio owner in the south to regularly use black and white singers and players together. There was a racial harmony among them unlike most other small southern towns in that day that lasted until the death of Martin Luther King Jr.

Talking about that dark day and how it affected the musicians, Rick put it this way on a PBS TV documentary: "Those pickers still played together after that, but the feeling of family just wasn't there any more."

Meanwhile, back in Jackson our group was floundering, even losing our disco gig. At least we didn't have to be "Slick" anymore.

Recording sessions were few and far between, and though that freed us to use the studio for our own music, the bills weren't getting paid.

Mike Daniel, in charge of the studio and a fine sound engineer, was hustling, trying to find some projects for us to play on, but most people that recorded in town went to the more popular Malaco Studios with now legendary producer and drummer James Stroud. (The first studio recording I ever played on was my Brother Neil's jazz album called "Stranger in a Foolish Land." We had recorded it several years earlier at Malaco.)

The desperate fiscal and musical silence was broken one spring evening as Mike announced to us that he had found us all a job… as the new "Fame Gang!" He had worked a deal with Rick Hall that would move us all up to Muscle Shoals to be the session musicians for Fame Studios. We would live in a trailer on Fame Ranch rent free, and get paid a salary plus union scale for the recording sessions that we played on.

Our ship had come in! We loaded up the van and we moved to… Alabama.

The Last Comet

It barely dampened our enthusiasm to find out after we moved in to the doublewide trailer on the ranch that the salary we thought would be $600 a month each was actually $600 a month *for the whole group*! We thought that we would soon be playing on a lot of hit records, writing our own hits, and making good money as session players.

Most musicians are dreamers and those dreams can keep hope alive even when the bills are slow in getting paid, at least for a while. I'm not saying that it's smart to be that way, but if we didn't love music so much most of us would be working "regular" jobs.

Even though my father had the experience of seeing his firstborn son, Neil, make his way as a professional musician (or maybe *because* of that!), he would occasionally ask me: "Son, don't you want to learn a trade so you will have something to fall back on?"

Keyboard synthesizers were becoming more vital in the pop sounds of the day. Chalmers Davis was older and more experienced with the synth - I played mostly piano. Also, Rick Hall had the strong conviction that younger players should have to "pay their dues," so I didn't get called for many union scale sessions.

I did, however, get to play piano on what became Bill Haley's last record. "Rock Around the Clock" was one of the first rock and roll hits of the '50's and launched Bill Haley and the Comets into orbit. In their day (the 1950's and early 60's), they were huge stars. They were mobbed at concerts and train stations by thousands of young admirers, much like the Beatles who rose to stardom after them. So I guess playing piano on his "London Sessions" in 1978 made me an honorary Comet.

Even years after his group broke up, Bill Haley was still selling records in Europe; that's why we were doing a new recording of his greatest hits. (I couldn't imagine going 20 years without writing and singing something new.) By this time, Bill Haley was well into his '60's, working on his third marriage and not appearing to be very happy. This experience showed me that fame wasn't all it was cracked up to be. He died not long after that recording.

I didn't really want to be famous, at least not so famous that I couldn't go to the grocery store without being mobbed (Okay, maybe once or twice would be fun). I think living in that kind of glass house would quickly turn the dream life into a nightmare… I mean, folks are *still* looking for Elvis!

No, I didn't want fame and I didn't really want to be rich. I just wanted to create and play good music for people that appreciated good music. I learned a lot working at Fame and got to write songs with writers such as Walt Aldridge (who later co-wrote many hits including "I Swear" recorded by a country star and later by NSync, or Boyz-To-Men, or the Backstreet Boys - one of those boy bands).

I sang on some demo sessions, and observed others, including some vocal sessions with Dobie Gray. Dobie and I hung out together some; I don't remember if I told him about singing his hit "Drift Away" as a teenager.

What a joy to see Dobie again a few years later when we sang together on the Bobby Jones Gospel television show. I was the white boy singing soulfully and moving stiffly! Bobby Jones, Dobie and I each took a verse of a rhythm and blues version of the hymn "Leaning on the Everlasting Arms".

I found out later that the savvy director had the camera do a close up on me when it was my verse so the "brothers" wouldn't make me look bad by their fluid movements!

By this time I was 21 years old. Even though I had had some exciting musical opportunities for one so young, still a gnawing restlessness haunted me.

-7-
<u>Sister Golden Hair Surprise</u>

"Her golden face was shining like the early morning sun

Within her blue eyes love clouds gently rained on everyone"

       Fame Studios was centrally located in Muscle Shoals. It was right behind Biscuit Village and only a short walk around the corner from the Kentucky Fried Chicken restaurant. I was car-less in those days, and frequently had the munchies due to a growing fondness for smoking pot. It was inevitable that I would eventually make my way toward the source of those mystical, wonderful, eleven herbs and spices wafting in the Alabama breeze.

       One of the first times I visited KFC, my friend, drummer Owen Hale from Lumberton, Mississippi accompanied me. Behind the counter of this well-run establishment was a vibrant, polite and pretty young lady. She was very professional and impressive as she took our orders. She had beautiful blue eyes and seemed very at peace with herself.

       I had a girlfriend at the time and things seemed to be headed in a serious direction with her, so I didn't pay quite as much attention as I would have were I unattached relationally speaking, but I did notice that this girl was striking.

My friend wanted to get her attention (and her phone number), so he used me to find out more about this mysterious, beautiful woman in the red KFC outfit.

Pointing in my direction Owen intoned. "He wants to take you out on a date," Owen said, as he elbowed me.

"Oh, really?" she smiled confidently.

"Yes, but he doesn't have a car," the drummer said with a smirk.

Without missing a beat the girl said, "That's O.K., I have a bike and he can help me pedal."

"Cute *and* spunky!" I thought.

"Yeah, that's no problem," I piped up.

"What are your names?" She asked.

I didn't realize it at the time, but with that brief conversation, a new chapter in my life began.

Lovely Rita

Her name was Rita Kaye Phillips, and she lived in nearby Sheffield, part of the Quad Cities that also included Tuscumbia (Helen Keller's birthplace), Florence, and Muscle Shoals.

Rita was a senior in high school and in addition to her studies and her restaurant job, she was president of the school choir, a youth leader and choir director at her church, and did much of the child care for her two younger brothers. Her mother, divorced, worked the second shift at the Ford plant. At this point in Rita's life, she rarely saw her father.

After getting to know Rita, she told me that when I first walked in to the restaurant where she worked, she elbowed her friend who also worked there and said, "Look at that guy, he's kinda' cute."

Her friend, who was also a member of her church, warned her. "Yes, but look at the redness in his eyes." (I was rather stoned at the time.)

There were several reasons that we had no business going out together. The main reason for me: I was practically engaged to a girl from Natchez who was attending school in Austin, Texas at the time. Lest you think I was totally disloyal, we had a crazy arrangement that, since we were apart, it was okay to go out with other people. I guess we were influenced by the Crosby, Stills, Nash, and Young song "Love the One You're With."

A Date With Density

Rita Phillips had her reasons not to date me as well. I was a pot-head. I was selfish and immature. Why, I didn't even wear socks! (Not to be fashionable, I just didn't care. It drove her mother nuts!) I was "kind-of" engaged. And the most serious obstacle of all, I was not a serious believer in Christ, and Rita was an ardent Christian.

I will never forget her driving us around on our dates. Though I didn't have wheels, hard-working Rita had bought her own powder blue Datsun B-210. I was glad we didn't have to take her bike.

On one of the first times we were together in the Datsun, I pulled a joint out of my pocket, as was my custom, to light it up and smoke it as we drove.

"What is that?" Rita asked.

"It's pot. Do you want some?" I responded.

"No I do not, and furthermore, you better get rid of that right now!"

It was a nice sized joint and I didn't want to get rid of it.

"You're kidding me, right?"

"No I am not, and if you don't throw it out of the window right now I am going to pull this car over and you can walk." She was serious and she told me later how much this incident had scared her.

I saw that she meant business, so after taking careful notice of our surroundings so I could retrieve it later, I rolled down the window and threw the marijuana out. (I never went back and got it.)

During one night out, we went back to the Fame trailer and I called my girlfriend - with Rita sitting right there! I didn't do it to be cool, I was just an idiot! What I didn't realize was that I was playing it just right without even knowing it.

You see, Rita had grown up being needed by everyone in her life. Her mother, Charlene, needed Rita to watch her younger brothers while she worked second shift at the Ford plant. Her brothers, Davy and Nolan needed her to be "Mom," and so identified Rita with that role that even with their real mother in the home 8 year-old Nolan still cried out for Rita first when he had a need for a drink of water, or a band-aid, or for help with his clothes.

As I said, she was the choir president at school, a youth director at her church, a responsible employee at KFC, a confidant to her friends, basically a strong person that people tended to lean on.

So when I came along giving her the illusion that I was strong and independent; this cute, hippy-jazz-rock musician that didn't seem to need her or anyone, she was hooked!

And so was I.

-8-

<u>Arrested</u>

The band wasn't working in the studio much. I was still writing songs and singing on demo sessions, but there was a general malaise inside my head and heart that seemed to be growing stronger.

A musician friend and I took a ride down to his folks' farm in Mississippi to harvest some pot plants. The drive took several hours during the heat of the summer. We loaded up (in more ways than one) and headed back to Muscle Shoals the same night, and under cover of darkness we transferred several dozen nice-sized cannabis plants into the house that we shared with a couple of other musicians.

For the next few weeks, I grew increasingly restless and paranoid. (Are you paranoid if they really *are* watching you?)

I tried several times, as I had in the past, to quit smoking pot. I remember one particularly intense effort as I rolled probably the biggest joint ever and scrawled on it: "The Last One."

It really *was* the last one… until the next one. I couldn't quit but I still refused to think of myself as anything other than a nice guy who smoked a little dope every now and then. At least I didn't steal anything (except the "roaches" - marijuana cigarette butts - out of my friends' ashtrays). Besides, if you asked me point blank, I would admit to being religious: "J.C.? He's cool."

One day in August, close to noon, I was having my usual breakfast of cereal and coffee alone in the house when a knock at the door shattered the silence.

At the door were three plainclothes policemen who had a warrant to search the house for drugs. Numbly, I opened the door and watched my life begin to change as they went through one room after another. They found less than an ounce in my room, but that was still enough to "haul me off" (to coin a Mississippi phrase) to the Colbert County jail.

My friend and partner in crime arrived just as we were leaving, so, rather than resist (the police had a warrant for his arrest), he wearily got into the back seat of the squad car with me.

We later found out that a retired police officer who lived right across the street from us happened to see us return from Mississippi that night with our fateful harvest. It turned out that the darkness didn't cover us quite as well as we had thought.

As we sat in the jail, one of the main things we feared was that Rick Hall was going to find out. Drinking in a dry county was one thing (after all, boys will be boys), but we had heard that our employer did not take kindly to drug trouble.

Somehow we only stayed in jail for about 6 hours, but that was enough for me not to want to make it a more permanent residence.

I borrowed the money for a lawyer from a friend, and found out that my trial was a month away. I was frightened and sobered by the situation.

Prayers Answered

I had spoken to Rita by phone a few times. She was friendly enough, but didn't give me the sympathy (or the lawyer's fees) that I was looking for. However, though I didn't know it until later, she did start praying for me with even more focus and fervency than she had before.

She prayed, not just that I wouldn't go to jail, but much more importantly, that I would find the peace and purpose in life that she sensed that I was desperate for. She also put her faith into action and invited me to her church. I finally said I would go, mostly so she would quit bugging me about it. Little did I know what I was in for!

The church she was a member of was a Pentecostal church, a Church of God. Other than the small African-American Baptist churches that my mother had taken me to when I was small, and playing bass for the Methodist youth group doing "Godspell" when I was 14, I had had very little experience with *protestant* churches, much less Pentecostal ones.

After fasting for three days Rita tried to prepare me for what she knew would be for me a new experience. Before we walked in she said, "Now David, I want you to know that we pray out loud." The only frame of reference I had was my own Catholic church experience so I answered, "That's O.K.; we prayed out loud too in the church I grew up in. We read the prayers out loud right from the prayer bulletins!" Have you guessed? That's right; this church didn't have prayer bulletins!

The people were friendly enough, greeting me warmly though they could tell by the way I was dressed and my lack of knowledge of the lingo they shared that I was obviously not one of their "tribe." Then the Pastor started the service: "Let us pray."

49.

And pray they did. Out LOUD - different prayers all at once! Almost everybody prayed fervently, loudly, all at the same time. If I was God, I would have gotten awfully confused.

Rita told me later that she was praying something like, "O Lord, help him understand." Being the reasonably intelligent person I was, I understood rather quickly that if God could hear us all pray different prayers *silently*, then what was so hard about Him hearing us pray out loud? Besides, the passion in the praying was intriguing to me, though the volume was overwhelming.

When the time came for singing hymns, I thought that the craziness was over. The hymnal was printed in English; the song leader looked like a man of great dignity. As he approached the platform, impeccably dressed in a three-piece suit, every white hair in place I thought, "This guy looks like he could really settle these crazy folks down." Then he started leading the song "Since Jesus Came into My Heart."

He started singing very loudly, jumping up and down with his face turning red, fists pumping in time to the piano and organ music. I looked around for the ushers because I thought he was having some sort of nervous breakdown. I just knew that others in the congregation would be mortified and embarrassed. These folks certainly weren't acting like we did in the church I grew up in.

As I looked around during the singing, I noticed that everyone else but me seemed to be getting into it and have no problem at all with the song leader's histrionics. In retrospect, I think of how excited folks get at a football game and how silly it really is on one level:

...the field has white lines dusted on it, the ball is a dead pig filled with air, and the players have these funny looking suits of armor, complete with helmets.

One guy yells, "hike!", and they all start bumping into each other, reaching for the pigskin. Finally, one of the guys catches the dead-pig ball and runs across a certain white line toward one end of the field, which causes mass hysteria and a celebration of momentous proportions.

Some men in the crowd even take their shirts off in mid-winter. They are wearing huge cheese-shaped wedges on their heads and are cheering wildly. Do they have a good reason for the raucous celebration?

Of course! After all, the dead pig has crossed THE line; lighted numbers have changed. Number "0" has become a "6," and all is right with the world!!

Again, I had tasted passion... reality and fervor and something (rather Someone) worth singing about - just as I had as a child in Natchez.

This time, however, I wanted to join in; I wanted to respond. I wanted to have something worth being this excited about.

After the music, I listened to the preacher speaking about the love that God has for us, that He demonstrated that love through Jesus Christ, that His death on a cross and His rising from the dead not only showed that He loved us, but that He had the power to give us new Life.

The speaker told us that we could actually have a loving, real relationship with the Creator of the universe instead of just giving Him lip-service. He said we could know a dynamic, personal God, instead of just going through the motions through obligatory church attendance to stay on His good side like I had experienced growing up.

As I listened intently, I flashed back to the times when I walked around Natchez as a lonely, awkward teenager just hoping that love was real and that I could know that love. It was like God was showing me to myself and showing Himself to me and offering me forgiveness, acceptance, peace, love, joy: everything that I had been looking for in music, girlfriends, popularity, weird philosophies, drugs and religion.

I found myself walking to the front of the church to pray. Before that night was over, I had become a new person in Jesus Christ. He changed my life and not only that, in profound ways that I didn't even begin to grasp just then, He had become my life!

A few days later at my trial, the felony I had been charged with was dropped to a misdemeanor and I got off with a $500 fine and probation.

Some might say, "David, what you got was just foxhole religion." Granted, my arrest and looming trial helped to show me what road I was on, but there is no doubt that I have been changed since that September night in Alabama.

Have I grown since then? I certainly hope so. The wonderful irony in "laying my life down for His sake" is that Jesus is helping me to be who I really am, much more "myself" than I ever would have been without Him.

And this formerly abused, messed-up, insecure young man actually is learning to know and love himself. I am free to be who I was originally created to be through Christ. And that is something worth celebrating!

Humpty Dumpty
David Baroni/ Bridge Builder Music/ BMI/ CCLI

Humpty Dumpty sat on a wall
Humpty Dumpty had such a terrible fall
That all the king's horses and all the king's men
Couldn't help old Humpty get it together again

With his life all in pieces he did the right thing
In the depths of his dilemma, he called on the king
Then the king said "Humpty, I've been watching you
Just waiting for this chance to pull you through" now

Humpty Dumpty's back together again
And he's happier now than he's ever been
Found his purpose for livin', his old life's forgiven
King Jesus came to his rescue
Made old Humpty Dumpty better than new...

...Once upon a time old Humpty was me
Then the King came along and He made me complete now

Humpty Dumpty's back together again
And I'm happier now than I've ever been
Found my purpose for livin', my old life's forgiven
King Jesus came to my rescue
Made this Humpty Dumpty better than new!

-9-
Segue

After the profound and wondrous feelings of my conversion waned a bit, I found that I had some questions about the whole thing.

"What happened?" I asked Rita.

"You got saved and sanctified and filled with the Holy Ghost," she replied.

Every answer seemed to generate more questions. I had many more to ask.

Rita and I began an intense few months of long walks, early morning Bible studies and times of prayer, followed by donuts and coffee (for me, that is; she, being more health conscious, drank orange juice).

After years of trying to quit smoking pot, I gave it up instantly and never looked back. I didn't even want it anymore. My language cleaned up too! For the first time in my life I had a sense of the nearness and realness of God and though I didn't know much, I knew somehow that He was real, and that He loved me and everybody else.

Rita helped so much in those early days and I found out only later how my questions had sent her scrambling to the

Bible or to prayer to find some answers. We became friends, then close friends, then… then I moved back to Natchez.

I had decided to leave what I considered at that time the "worldly" studio scene and just write "Christian" music. Rita and I said sad goodbyes and promised to keep in touch through letters and the occasional phone call. I hopped on the Greyhound bus that took my saved self back to Mississippi.

It's A Different World

Conversations around the dining room table of my childhood were as diverse as the books that spilled over the shelves that lined the hallways in our home on Monroe Street. As I've mentioned there were books by authors from avant-garde psychiatrist Carl Jung to feminist Erica Jong; from obscure Catholic theological tomes (left there by a friend of the family who had left the priesthood) to the irreverent humor of beat-comedian Lenny Bruce.

There was even a copy of the Communist Manifesto and Mao's Little Red Book (for educational purposes only, of course). From Jung to Jong to Tung (say *that* three times), the cornucopia of books and magazines in the hallway of our family home mirrored in some ways the rapidly changing world of the 1960's and '70's.

The home of my childhood also brimmed with scintillating conversations that were enriched by the out-of-town and local guests that frequented our backyard patio. These visitors (some became houseguests for days and weeks at a time) were drawn there by my mother's reputation as a brave Caucasian housewife leader in the Civil Rights movement. (Once I asked visiting luminary Dorothy Day if I could blow her grits to cool them down!)

Certain terms have particularly loaded connotations - like the terms "Liberal" or "Conservative." In retrospect, it doesn't take a lot of deductive powers to see that my family of origin was, in that day, decidedly and unabashedly liberal. Combine that political persuasion with the Catholic religious bent of my parents, and it was no surprise that my conversion (and vocal proclamation of it) caused no lack of consternation to my family. I considered myself converted to Christ - they saw it as being converted to brainless Protestantism. (In retrospect, we were both right in some ways.)

At first they assumed that I had been brainwashed by a pretty girl and had, at her enticement, joined a cult. After they met Rita and observed her down-to-earth demeanor they saw that she was reasonably sane and only a bit overzealous, and concluded that I alone had gone nuts.

My sister Rose Ann, in particular, thought it highly peculiar that when I moved out of the studio scene back to Monroe Street, my daily morning ritual consisted of reading the Bible while I ate my cereal. I still remember the look of incredulity on her face when she described that scene later saying: "There you were, every day, eating your cereal and reading *the Bible!*"

Granted, my behavior had certainly changed, and I didn't have a lot of wisdom to match my newfound zeal, but God had definitely made Himself real to me like I had never experienced before, and I wanted to share my new faith.

I had a lot of spare time in those months in Natchez. I wrote some songs, grew in my relationship with the Lord, and took many walks down by the Mississippi River. I also fought boredom and depression, and I didn't have many outlets for my creativity.

While I had been working at Fame studios, I had signed a

five-year exclusive songwriter's contract. This meant that any song I wrote for the duration of the contract was the property of Fame Publishing, even though I no longer worked at the studio.

One day, on a whim, I sent a cassette demo of a few songs I had written to Mike Daniel, my sound engineer friend from the studio in Muscle Shoals. He forwarded the tape to Nashville producer Boomer Castleman, who in turn played the tape for an eccentric genius songwriter and producer named Gary S. Paxton.

I got a call from Paxton who introduced himself, complimented the songs, and asked if I had any others. We made arrangements for me to go to Nashville to meet him and play him some of my new songs. I left the driving to Greyhound again, and got my songwriting self back on the bus; this time to Nashville.

Music City U.S.A.

Gary S. Paxton (he says, "Don't forget the "S;" it is one-third of my whole name") was a trip! Producer of such novelty hits as "Monster Mash" and "Long-Haired Flying Purple People Eater," Gary had come to know the Lord after a long bout with alcoholism, 7 or 8 failed marriages, and the precarious ups and downs of the music industry. His genius for thought-provoking lyrics and innovative production ideas was almost too radical for the fledgling contemporary Christian music scene.

In the Wax Works recording studio, nestled in the residential Berry Hill neighborhood in Nashville, I sat at the piano and played and recorded demos of some of the songs I had just written. Gary liked what he heard and began to tell me of his plans to produce a record for me, to get me and my songs heard on the radio and Christian TV. The ideas were coming fast and furious and we were getting excited.

Then I remembered the Fame contract and told Gary about it.

"So technically these aren't your songs," he said.

Crestfallen, I mumbled, "I guess not."

Undaunted, Gary said, "Then, why don't you ask Fame to let you out of the contract since you are just writing Christian songs now and they don't have much interest in those kind of songs?"

So I did just that. I asked them to let me out of the contract.

Within a few months, they did (this was almost unheard of)! I was back in Natchez when I got the phone call that I had been released from the contract. I loaded up my worldly goods (it took me about 5 minutes), said goodbye to my parents and some friends, got on the bus (yet again), and moved to Nashville, "Music City, USA" to start work on my first album.

-10-
Berry Hill

After staying with a friend from back home for a week or so, and staying a few nights at the fabulous 12 Oaks Motel in beautiful downtown Berry Hill (actually it was a decent motel), record producer Gary Paxton helped me get into a one bedroom apartment close to the studio by cosigning the lease.

I moved in with all my worldly possessions: some china dishes that my mother had given me, my Yamaha CP-70 electric grand piano, an acoustic guitar, my stereo system and a cardboard box that served as my dining room table. Some friends at church gave me a twin bed. I was all set to make music!

Gary Paxton was a wonderful, though eccentric, producer. I thought I knew how to sing until I worked with him.

He would make me sing a line over and over in the studio:
"You're flat, sing it again."
"The pitch was good, but I didn't believe you."

"That was a little sharp, but I like the conviction and passion in your voice. We'll slap some reverb on it and it will be fine."

I got to play with some of the finest session musicians in Nashville, folks like legendary session drummer, Kenny Malone, bass player Gary Lunn (who was my age), and Dan Huff, the phenomenal guitarist who is one of the most sought after producers on the music scene to this day.

The album that I thought would take 2 months to record took 2 years instead. Because I wasn't yet signed to a label, Gary S. Paxton spent his own money on the production. We had to wait for his quarterly royalty checks to come in to spend more on the recording. Gary spared no expense.

We had strings or horns - the real thing, not synthesizers - on most of the songs, and the mixes and arrangements were sparkling, honest, and fresh. I have done many studio records since then, but none had the time and expense of that first album.

Rita and I had decided to end the serious part of our relationship and be "just friends." We communicated some, mostly through letters. I let her little brother Davy come and spend a couple of weeks with me in the summertime. We played a lot of sock basketball in my tiny apartment.

The Sheffield youth choir invited me to join them and play and sing for an upcoming performance they were having back in Alabama.

Rita still directed the choir so we got together to talk about the music. One thing led to another and before our conversation was over, we were talking about getting married! There was an unmistakable bond between us that went deeper than friendship.

We set a wedding date. We moved it up twice before finally deciding on November 1st, 1980. It was time to talk to my future mother-in-law (gulp).

Charlene Robinson Phillips was, in many ways, an imposing woman. She grew up in bloody Harlan County in Kentucky. Her mother was a hard-core Pentecostal woman whose demeanor made it appear that she thought that having fun must be a sin.

Charlene had had a rough marriage to Bobby Phillips. They divorced then remarried each other but couldn't make it work and divorced again. Bobby was a sometimes volatile alcoholic, and that didn't do much to help Charlene have trust and respect for men in general.

When we announced our plans for marriage, Charlene took me aside and said, "Now David, there are men that would work three jobs for Rita and you are living in Nashville, waiting on your musical dream to come true, but you don't have a job." (I was living a rather Spartan existence, depending on help from my producer to pay the rent.)

She continued, "Maybe if you would get a job and show the Lord that you are willing to work outside of music, He might just bless the music side of it too."

Actually, she was right.

So when I traveled back to Nashville, I brought my paucity of workforce experience right into Krystal Hamburgers. I immediately got hired for the graveyard shift; then I walked a few more blocks to Wendy's Hamburgers and got hired for the lunch rush.

I was the "side-change" drive thru window person at both restaurants and also the grill man at Wendy's. I know where the meat for Wendy's Chili comes from (don't panic, it comes from the hamburger patties that have been on the grill for a certain time without being sold). The manager would come by, point at a few of those burgers and say, "Chili meat." Then I would scoop them up with my spatula and deposit them in the chili meat bucket.

I am grateful for that "real-world" work experience. I even excelled at cooking the Krystal breakfasts. Actually, they have a fool-proof system. If I could do it anyone can. I have fond memories of the late-night customers that came in for breakfast after the bars closed. Not abandoning music, I wrote a few songs on Krystal hamburger bags.

One night a customer drove through the drive through with his car reeking of pot. I thought that perhaps my former lifestyle had equipped me to talk to him about the love of God so I asked him if he ever read the Bible, or if he believed in God. With slurred speech and blurred vision he smiled at me and said, "Who, J.C.? He's cool!"

After Rita and I got married, I did concerts occasionally; I worked on the album, wrote songs, and eventually settled into a job as a laborer on a concrete construction crew.

A man at our church hired me, even though I didn't know what a two-by-four was. My first day on the job, he sent me around the back of the house we were working on to bring him a two-by-four. I didn't have the guts to admit to him that I didn't know what that was, so I walked around back.

I don't know if I expected the item in question to be labeled or what, but after a futile search I finally had to come back around to the front of the house and admit my ignorance. The crew laughed about that good-naturedly for years.

That work experience has helped me to relate to people in the "real world" and has proved to be invaluable.

One day on a driveway job I was using a buck-knife to open a bucket concrete sealer and the knife snapped closed on the knuckle of my right forefinger. (Remember, I am a piano

62.

player. My hands, however, were not insured by Lloyd's of London.)

My boss was on another job at the time and didn't realize how severely I had cut my finger, so he took his time returning for me and driving me to the hospital. I received quite a few stitches and had to wear a "Captain Hook" looking kind of brace over my finger.

I played piano with it like that for a few weeks, doing pretty basic right-hand playing, until the brace was finally removed. I have a souvenir scar on my right forefinger to this day to remind me of the hazards of my former "day-job."

So here we were, the happy young newlyweds. I had muscles from my concrete work; I was suntanned and sleeping good at night. Life was good, marriage was great!

Only it wasn't.

One night, while I was still working down the street at Krystal and Rita was in our apartment alone, a strange man knocked at the door of our apartment. He looked like a drug dealer and scared Rita (we didn't live in the best part of Nashville anyway).

She hurriedly dressed, and when she thought it was safe, she made a dash to our car, a baby blue 1978 Datsun B210.

"Hey you!" the man yelled.

Trembling, Rita made it to the car, drove the half block down the street to Krystal where I was blissfully serving the small hamburgers to the late night clientele.

Rita rushed in in tears and ran straight to the ladies room.

After about 20 minutes, I thought I better find out was going on. As she poured out her story I realized that the incident with the scary drug-dealer stranger was just the tip of the iceberg for Rita (I'm a bit embarrassed as I think about the blissful insensitivity that I had early in our marriage, but it is part of my story).

As I mentioned, we lived in a rundown part of town. I worked nights and Rita worked days, so we didn't have much quality time together. Rita was a trooper and rarely complained, but in those early years we didn't have a phone, our apartment got robbed twice, and worst of all, I spiritualized everything.

Instead of sitting down and having a heart-to-heart conversation with my bride, I would just say, "Let's pray about it."

I didn't realize how afraid I was of real intimacy; I honestly thought I was doing the right thing. She had married a performing robot who thought he was real.

Rita, at the tender age of nineteen, had moved away from a supportive group of friends and her vibrant church to Nashville where she knew no one. Combine that with my insensitivity to her feelings and my blissful ignorance about married life, and Rita was not a happy camper.

We somehow survived the incident with the strange man coming to the door, but the last straw concerning our first apartment appeared in the form of a little furry creature - a mouse in the kitchen.

Rita could handle not having a phone. She even tolerated the two break-ins, and the stranger knocking on the door. But when one of Mickey's cousins twittered and scampered around the kitchen, that was it.

We moved in to a basement at a friend's house for a month or two, and then found our own duplex to rent.

After two years of working and waiting, finally my first album was released. Gary Paxton wanted to title it, "The Legend of David Baroni: Volume 1." He was serious.

As flattering as that was, I thought that title would be perceived as arrogant, so after much conversation back and forth, we finally agreed to call it, "From the Heart." I didn't totally win the naming battle however, because Gary stubbornly had the graphic designer add, "The Legend of David Baroni: Volume 1" to the back cover!

One of the songs from that project called "Soldier of the Light" was recorded by Andrus-Blackwood and Company, a popular group at that time. The song promptly went to Number One on the Contemporary Christian Music radio airplay charts and stayed there for six months!

When it was nominated for a Dove Award for Song of the Year I thought, "Man, this Christian music thing is easy!" There were some exciting musical milestones in those early days. And I had a lot of growing up to do.

-11-
New Beginnings

As I achieved a measure of success as a songwriter and recording artist, there was a part of me that was afraid that being successful in the gospel music industry would cause me to compromise my convictions.

There were (and are) some wonderful people involved in all facets of the Christian music world. However, because there is money and power and fame involved, there is also the same sordid, sleazy side that is sometimes evident in the music business at large.

I was part of a denomination that prided itself on its "holiness" and "separation from the world," and though I didn't realize it then, I had a judgmental, prideful attitude that I tried to hide behind a sanctimonious smile. I meant well, but I didn't realize then how small and uptight my view of God was. Though in some ways I was a man of faith, most of the time I lived in fear.

I was like one of the dwarves in C.S. Lewis's "The Chronicles of Narnia." In his wonderful story of Aslan the Lion and the land of Narnia, there was a time when some fearful dwarves hid in a cave because they were being pursued by warriors sent by the evil White Witch.

From time to time evil imposters sent by the enemy came to the mouth of the cave and pretended to be Aslan, the good King of Narnia. The dwarves were desperately afraid of being deceived so they stayed in the relative safety of their cave.

Then came the day when Aslan Himself actually came to the mouth of the cave to announce that the war was over, and that he had come to set them free from the dark, dank cave.

Having cultivated the habit of being suspicious, they were afraid that it was another trick. They didn't recognize the voice of the benevolent Lion King, and they chose to stay in the cave.

I'm sad to say that I had that attitude for awhile about not only the music business, but about life.

Unfortunately I was praised and applauded by most of the people close to me for my "uncompromising" stand. They were just doing what they thought was right.

Of course now I have the perspective of many years of hindsight. You can only glean from experience by either going through adversity yourself, or by learning and listening to the wisdom of others who have been there before you. For a long time I didn't know anybody like that that I dared to trust, so I remained in the cave.

I try not to give myself a hard time about my immaturity and where I was because, as Rita says, "you can't see what you can't see, and you don't know what you don't know."

It wasn't all gloom and doom and dour religiosity. I am grateful for the many wonderful, humble, and loving people I met in the church in which we were a part. I learned a lot of good things too. Many of those folks modeled integrity, commitment, and a healthy fear of the Lord. I also had a blast in the studio working on my first album. Michelangelo can have the Sistine Chapel ceiling - give me the opportunity to create in a recording studio.

Concerts were fun and meaningful. I had a lot of energy and moved back and forth behind the piano kind of like Ray Charles. It wasn't anything intentional, I just had a bad case of the "I-can't-help-its." The music I wrote, while pop-flavored, was jazzy and fresh, especially for the early years of what was starting to be called Contemporary Christian Music.

Artists and musicians like Russ Taff, The Imperials, Phil Driscoll, and Debby Boone really liked my songs. Phil Driscoll and Debby Boone won a Grammy for their vocal version of a song I co-wrote with Connie Nelson called "Keep the Flame Burning." It was a thrill to meet her and one of my favorite bass players, Abraham Laboriel, backstage at her concert in Nashville.

At my own concerts I signed autographs. I heard myself singing on the radio. Some of my songs climbed the charts. I signed an exclusive songwriting contract with Word Music and received a mind-boggling advance of $12,000! Meadowgreen Music had also wanted me to sign with them (Michael W. Smith and Gary Chapman had just signed with that publishing company), so that gave me some negotiating leverage with Word. They probably would have offered me a much lower advance otherwise.

The advance money reminded me of that first band gig when I was twelve years old. Wow, money to make music!

With our newfound "wealth," Rita and I went car shopping. We were so naïve that we paid a car dealership a huge down payment and practically begged them to let us have the car at sticker price (never again…).

However, in spite of all the success I achieved, I still wasn't sure that I should be full time in music until a pastor friend, Terry Lineberry, gave me some great advice. As we were discussing whether or not I should be a full time musician-songwriter-recording artist, Terry put it this way: "David, why don't you go full-time for two years and at the end of that time, evaluate where you are and see if God has blessed your doing that? Otherwise you are going to wonder for the rest of your life if you should have gone for it."

That made good sense to me, so in January of 1984 Rita and I hit the road in our newly purchased 1982 Aries K-Car with our three week old firstborn, Bethany Rozan in tow.

Fatherhood

Rita and I had talked about waiting five years or so before having children, but Bethany had a plan of her own.

It had been an unusually cold winter in Nashville. After moving five times we settled in to a duplex on Cedarmont Drive. I was across town with a friend when Rita's water broke while she watched Hee Haw (she didn't make a habit of watching that show, but she was pregnant and uncomfortable and we didn't have remotes or cable TV back then).

I got home right before a friend came to take her to the hospital. We didn't have cell phones back then, so I had had no way of knowing that Bethany was on her way. She was 3 weeks early. I am glad I didn't miss the drive to the hospital.

I asked Rita if I had time to take a shower before leaving for the hospital. Since she hadn't had any contractions yet, my calm, cool, and collected wife said, "Sure."

While I was in the shower, the first labor pain, a big one, hit her.

"DAVID! GET OUT OF THE SHOWER; WE'VE GOT TO GO NOW!"

Never have I been so nervous and received so many contrary driving instructions as I did that night driving Rita to the hospital.

"Hurry up!"

"Run that red light!"

"SLOW DOWN those are railroad tracks!"

"Don't you see the red light? Stop!"

Thankfully, we survived the trip downtown.

Once we arrived, Rita calmly checked herself in to the maternity ward while I parked the car. She was so calm that the hospital attendant had difficulty believing that our daughter's birth was imminent.

"How do you know you are going to have a baby?"

"Because my water broke an hour ago."

"And?"

"And because my contractions are 4 minutes apart."

Refusing to be impressed with that, the lady said again: "And?"

This kind of made Rita upset (she is pretty good at knowing her body, and her self-diagnosis is usually uncannily accurate), so she said, "At my last doctor visit I had dilated to 4!"

"Oooh child, we better get you to a birthing bed!"

Less than an hour and a half after arriving at the hospital, Rita gave birth to a 6 pound, 11 ounce, dark haired, beautiful bundle of joy that we named Bethany Rozan. I marveled at this tiny life, this precious girl as I held her for the first time. Her tiny fingers and toes, her helplessness and her strength, this child that I was already in love with rested trustingly in my arms. I was a father.

That night I started a song to Bethany that Rita helped me finish. It was a blessed collaboration in two ways.

"Bethany Rozan"
(David and Rita Baroni/Kingdomsongs Inc./BMI)

Bethany, Bethany
You're precious to your daddy and me
You're so full of life and full of love
Bethany, Bethany
You're the beautiful melody
In a song that has been given from above

Bethany Rozan
We'll do all we can to show we love you
Bethany so sweet
You make our lives complete
And we thank our God above
For sending you our precious love
We love you Bethany

Bethany, Bethany
You look like daddy, you look like me
You're our special gift from God you see
Bethany, Bethany
Welcome to the family
Jesus smiles upon us

Bethany Rozan
We'll do all we can to show we love you
Bethany so sweet
You make our lives complete
And we thank our God above
For sending you our precious love
We love you Bethany

As we traveled, mostly by car in that first couple of years, almost everywhere we went we sang Bethany's song to her in concert. Years later, several people have told us how much seeing our family together meant to them. Some even named their daughters Bethany. It wasn't always easy to travel together, especially for Rita having to take care of an infant.

One time we were housed at a church "guest room" in Illinois, to save the church the expense of a hotel room. Imagine our surprise to be awakened by loud, "Pentecostal" praying at 5 a.m. the next morning; we were right next to the prayer room for these fervent folks. Talk about ambivalence - I felt angry that they were praying so loud that they woke me and my bride and our baby at such an early hour. Then again, they were so fervent in their praying that I felt guilty for not joining them.

Ah, but those inconveniences make for great stories now. All in all, I have a lot of wonderful memories from those early days.

When Bethany was just 13 months old, Rita, Bethany and I were gathered with other family members in Rita's sister Frieda's apartment for a special occasion: The Grammy Awards.

Bethany was just in the process of taking her very first steps when they announced on TV that Debby Boone and Phil Driscoll had won the Grammy for best vocal by a duo or group for my song, "Keep the Flame Burning." Rita screamed in excitement, Bethany screamed in terror, fell on her bottom, and didn't try to walk again for another month!

The local paper in my hometown did a story about how proud my family in Natchez was that I had been honored with the Grammy award. The headline was something like "Local Family Basks in Grammy Glory." On the day the story came out, my mother called Nannie to ask what she was doing and Nannie replied in her inimitable way, "Oh, I'm just over here basking in Grammy glory."

I have appreciated the sense of humor that I inherited from both sides of my family tree. Once after a ball game, my brother Mark and I asked our older brother Neil what he felt like eating. He formed a big circle by putting his arms over his head and dead-panned, "I feel like a pizza."

After the first few years of being terminally serious in my concerts, I finally started loosening up. I figured that if I was going to do this for a large part of my life, I was going to enjoy myself. People seem to enjoy my humor, but probably not as much as I do. I will laugh at myself even if others don't.

-12-
Double Blessing

Rita was five months pregnant. She and Bethany and I were in Newport News, Virginia when she began to have cramps and bleeding. After a call to Rita's doctor in Nashville, we began the long ride home, stopping every few hours for Rita to try to get comfortable. When we arrived in Nashville, she went to see the doctor. It was not good news.

Sadly, Rita had a miscarriage within a few days.

We had already faced some adversity in our marriage: some financial struggles, the death of Rita's grandmother, the difficulty of adjusting to married life that most young couples face.

My favorite way to deal with trouble was to pretend it wasn't there (If I put my hands over my eyes, maybe you won't be able to see me). I tried praying things away or spiritualizing them with a weird combination of faith and fatalism. After a season of grieving the miscarriage, I naively became convinced that one child must be all we were supposed to have.

Bethany was our pride and joy, and Rita did an exceptional job of teaching her. Instead of just saying "See the ball?" Rita would say, "Bethany, do you see the round red big ball?"

Today Bethany has a great vocabulary and is a gifted communicator and songwriter. Bethany sang (in tune!) on her first recording at age three. What a joy she is to Rita and me.

Thankfully she doesn't have a morbid fear of water. Let me explain.

We were in Hawaii for some concerts and Mommy, Daddy, and Baby were playing in the ocean. Bethany and I were having a great time playing catch - she was the beach ball. I would throw her up in the air and catch her just as her feet splashed in the waves. We did this successfully about a dozen times and had gotten so good at it, I wanted to show Rita.

"Look Mommy!" I yelled as I threw Bethany up real high to impress both of the women in my life. Only this time, I didn't catch her. She plunged beneath the surf at Ala Moana Beach. Frantically I searched for her, grabbed her and picked her up, while she spluttered and cried. For some reason Mama Rita was not very impressed.

Neither was Bethany.

Then there was the time when Bethany realized that sometimes Daddies can't keep their promises. She was 13 or 14 by this time and really into roller-blading. She was poised at the top of our driveway in Franklin, ready to race down to me while I waited at the bottom (at the time this seemed like a dandy idea to both of us).

"Daddy will you catch me?"

"Sure baby, I will catch you." (How hard could this be?)

Perhaps subliminally remembering the beach fiasco long ago, she asked me again, "Are you sure Dad?"

Getting a little miffed that my fatherly prowess was in question I replied: "Of course I will catch you sweetheart."

"Dad, do you promise?"

"Yes honey, I promise."

Fortified with my earnest reassurances, she took a deep breath, trusted her father, and launched herself from the top of the driveway straight toward me.

Down she comes.

"I've got you… I've got you…umph!!"

You guessed it, dad and daughter tumbled over each other; fortunately Bethany wasn't hurt badly, at least not physically (she has since assured me that she has worked through those traumas).

Surprise!

We did some concerts in the Los Angeles area and visited with our friends Craig and Dianne Andrus for a few days. Rita and Dianne went shopping while Craig and I rode his motorcycles and enjoyed the coastal breeze and the southern California sun.

When the girls returned, Rita started showing me some of her purchases. I listened half-heartedly (clothes have never been very interesting to me) as she showed me a dress and a nice blouse or two. Then she held up some pants. She said nonchalantly, "I can wear these in a few months when I start showing." She continued the conversation until I stopped her with a double take.

"What did you say?"

"You heard me; you are going to be a daddy again!"

After I processed the initial shock, I was ecstatic.

On Feb. 8, 1987, Rita was calmly timing her contractions during the Sunday evening worship service. Afterward we were visiting with some of our friends at a restaurant when Rita got that certain look on her face (remember, she is very in touch with her body). It was time to go to the hospital, baby time!

Only it wasn't quite time.

Rita had been in the hospital barely over an hour when Bethany was born. This birth was taking a bit longer. At about midnight, Dr. Netherton was just about to send us home when she decided just to be safe that we should stay the night.

Typical male that I am, I almost complained about how uncomfortable it was to sleep in the lounge chair by Rita's bed. Those noisy nurses kept coming in all night to check on my wife and kept waking me up. Fortunately for me I was smart enough to keep my whining to myself.

The sun rose, no baby yet. I was tired… and hungry.

I asked Rita if she was okay and if she would mind if I went and grabbed a fast breakfast. She cheerfully bid me go (glad to be rid of me for a while, I'm sure).

I returned to the hospital satisfied from a fine Hardee's steak and biscuit with grape jelly. There was an increase in the intensity level in the maternity ward. While I was gone, Dr. Netherton had broken Rita's water and it was "go time."

I rushed into my scrubs, typical modesty thrown to the winds as I undressed and dressed in front of the medical staff (who didn't notice).

Rita was in more than the normal pain and asked for medicine. It was then that she remembered her vow not to have natural childbirth any more after she had had Bethany that way.

Dr. Netherton told her that it was too late for meds, and that the baby was crowning. It would be over in a little while. "Just push!" she said.

As she grabbed my arm and pulled me over to her during a contraction, almost knocking the IV pole over, Rita did just that. She pushed.

At 9:17 a.m. on February 9th, Rita gave birth to a 5 lb. 2 oz baby girl. We named her Charity Lynne, and she was a beauty! I was fawning over her and taking pictures when I heard Rita telling the doctor that she still had some pain in her back.

"Don't worry honey, that's just the afterbirth. Rest a few minutes and we will take care of that."

Then the doctor said something I will never forget. In a voice filled with amazement, the capable and professional Dr. Netherton said, "Lord, I don't believe it, there is another baby in there!"

Stunned, I said "You're kidding."

Very soberly she replied, "No."

Rita cried out to the doctor, "Then you're gonna have to get it out, or give me an epidural or something 'cause I'm done!"

Eight or nine minutes later, 4 lb. 9 oz Celeste Gabrielle was born. They were the first surprise twins in Williamson County in five years.

Rita was the talk of the hospital. Her own mother called her a liar when Rita called her to tell her that she had had not one baby girl, but two!

A kindergarten teacher knocked on my sleepy, delirious, wife's hospital door to ask if her class could come in and see the mother of the surprise twins. All 15 of them piled in and sang a song to Rita about 10 ducks in the water. One swam away and then there were nine and then... on and on it went.
It was the longest song in the history of maternal recuperation, but Rita laid there and smiled until the lonely end (she thought those ducks would never all swim away).

Thank God for our friends at church who bought an extra crib and other things, and helped us out in those first crazy, wonderful, wearying weeks. Though Charity and Celeste were five weeks premature, they were healthy and came home after only one extra day in the hospital.

Of course, we wrote a song for them as well:

Charity and Celeste
David and Rita Baroni/ Kingdomsongs Inc./ BMI/CCLI

Charity Lynne, where do we begin
To tell you of our love
Celeste Gabrielle, our little angel
Sent to us from God above

We'll kiss away your tears
Protect you from your fears
And love you through the years
We'll watch you while you play
Teach you how to pray
And guide you on your way

Charity Lynne, where do we begin
To tell you of our love
Celeste Gabrielle, our little angel
Sent to us from God above

And now we give you to
The One Who gave us you
Abundantly we're blessed
With Bethany, Charity and Celeste

We quickly got into a rhythm. Rita nursed, but I still got to be involved in the care of our girls. She would feed one twin, I would burp her and change her and put her to bed, go to sleep for about 10 minutes until the other twin awoke. Rita would feed her, I would burp her and change her and put her back to bed. In 2 hours or so, we would do it all again.

Sometimes when I would be on the road (after all, the light bill and the mortgage had to be paid), Rita would come down after a virtually sleepless night and find her uneaten dinner sitting in a plate on top of the microwave and not remember how it got there.

Bethany was a great big sister. She even learned to change diapers when she was barely 3 and-a-half years old.

I used to love holding Charity on one shoulder (side-saddle), Celeste on the other, and Bethany hanging on to my back. I felt like Super Dad.

Rita surprised me in California with the news that we were going to have a baby, and God surprised us all when we had two-for-the-price-of-one: a double blessing.

After Rita shared our "surprise twins" story one night in a concert, Celeste, who was four years old at the time, spoke up.

"It hurts my feelings when you say that I am a surprise."

Rita quickly and wisely responded, "Oh sweetheart, it's like the best kind of surprise, like at Christmas time when you get something you really wanted but weren't expecting. You are the best kind of surprise."

Charity and Celeste were very close (they still are), but they were not without their moments of discord.

Once when Rita and I were out of town, we left the girls with Rita's mother, whom we called "Granny." As Granny was giving the 3 year old twins a bath, she left them in the tub to answer a plea for help in the kitchen from Bethany.

Though she only left them for a few moments, she was alarmed to hear an inordinate amount of splashing as she hurriedly returned to the bathroom just in time to see Charity with her hands around her sister's throat, choking her.

"Charity, you are going to kill Sissy!"

Charity let go and calmly answered her grandmother: "Oh no Granny, I'm not going to kill Celeste, I'm just going to hurt her!"

Our children, now grown, have told us things that have happened - like one of them pushing the other down a flight of stairs and then swearing her to secrecy - that I am glad I didn't know about until now (come to think of it, I probably have some boyhood adventures that I need to tell my dad about).

A Sobering Diagnosis

We have a picture of Charity and Celeste in the hallway of our home that shows them in their high chairs on their one year birthday. Charity is sitting up straight, excited for the cake that she is about to tear into. Celeste, however, is leaning over sideways, and the tray of the high chair is pressed right up against her chest to keep her from falling over. We didn't think much about that at the time, but now the photograph has a lot of significance to our family.

When the twins were 13 months old, they had very different physical abilities. Charity was almost walking by this time; Celeste couldn't even crawl. She would pull herself along with her arms, army style. Charity could zoom up a flight of stairs; Celeste couldn't sit up in the high chair without help.

We had heard that twins develop at different rates, so we tried not to be overly concerned, but by that age we suspected something was wrong with Celeste.

We took her to our pediatrician who soberly referred us to a neurologist who informed us that Celeste had Cerebral Palsy, probably from a twisted umbilical cord in the womb. She sent us across town for a brain scan. We were numb, we were devastated.

Rita was so upset (she is usually very capable and calm in times of crisis), that she couldn't go in to the room that contained the Star Wars-like tube that Celeste would be placed in for the MRI scan. It was surreal for me to hold my infant daughter. I was afraid and prayerful and somewhat numb as I gave her the milk and medicine-filled bottle that would put her to sleep so that she would be still for the test.

After receiving the diagnosis, Rita checked into physical and occupational therapy for Celeste, and we also talked about things like wheelchairs for children. We were told that Celeste would probably never walk and certainly never run. It was a sobering time filled with a lot of prayer and a lot of fear and sadness.

After a particularly trying day, Rita found herself in the bathroom, her favorite praying place. It was the only place she could have privacy with three small children in the house. She remembers telling God, "Lord, I don't care if Celeste never walks on earth as long as I know she is going to run in heaven." Celeste had army-crawled into the bathroom by this time. Rita picked her up and Celeste began playing with her Mommy's tears. My devastated wife continued the prayer, "Lord, Your Word says that your grace is sufficient and I just need an abundance of your grace right now."

Right after she said that, she felt the honey-like peace and presence of God from the top of her head through her whole body.

Within a few days, Rita had taken Celeste back to the physical therapy nurse for the painful process of working out the stiffness in Celeste's little-used muscles. It was so traumatic for Rita to hear her baby crying in pain that she usually waited out in the hallway until the session was over.

In a short while, the nurse came out carrying Celeste. She said to Rita, "Did you bring me the wrong twin?" (She thought Rita was playing a joke on her.)

"No, that is Celeste."

"Well, if this is Celeste then I don't know what to tell you; there is nothing wrong with this child."

Rita remembered that for about 5 days in a row, Celeste had done something different each day that she had never been able to do before. Finally she dared to voice her conviction.

"I think the Lord has healed Celeste."

The nurse replied, "I think so too because there is nothing wrong with her muscles; she is not even tight any more!"

We got a call from the neurologist. "Mrs. Baroni, we looked at the brain scan and we can't find a thing wrong with your daughter."

Celeste was totally healed by the Lord! She became a state champion gymnast along with her sister Charity. Celeste excelled in the parallel bars, which requires tremendous coordination and upper body strength. In her senior year of high school, Celeste was the first female to win the top Athlete/Academic award.

Sometimes when the girls were younger, Celeste would do things like talk to a perfect stranger in a swimming pool and say, "Jesus healed me of Cerebral Palsy when I was a baby. Tell her, Mom."

Rita got to tell a lot of people that story and now Celeste tells it herself.

I don't know why God chose to show His love to us by healing Celeste. I know that many times people ask God and are not healed. We are certainly not any more deserving of His healing than anyone else. I do know that, whether or not the healing comes, somehow God's grace really is enough.

-13-
Living in Color

I have learned a lot through the songs that I have been given. A dear friend of mine is Morris Chapman. In the early 80's we had the same record producer. Morris is one of those rare, exceptionally gifted brothers with a passion for the Lord, and a unique musical style that comes from the heart.

At 40 years old, Morris quit his job as a high school janitor in Las Vegas and become a world renowned recording artist and songwriter. Ever aware that God is his source of inspiration, He calls songwriters "song receivers." I think that is an apt description.

The same year that our twins were born, 1987, I was in Wichita, Kansas. I was scheduled to sing at a big youth convention. By this time I had been traveling full time in music for over three years, and things were going well in my career. People were buying my albums and hearing my songs on the radio. I got to co-write with Dove Award winning songwriters like Niles Borop and Regie Hamm (I had been Regie's camp counselor at a youth camp just a few years earlier). My concert schedule was full, and finances were in good shape. Yet, I was unsettled.

So as I drove the rental car to the venue in Wichita, I had a little talk with God:

"God, what did You put me here for?"

He answered me. Not in an audible voice - it was much louder than that.

"Do you want to know what I have called you to do?" (Have you ever noticed that a lot of time before God answers, He asks some questions Himself? And many times they seem like questions with very obvious answers. Sometimes I feel like responding, "Well duh, I just *asked* You to tell me what you wanted me to do!")

So I answered, "Yes Lord, I'm ready. Tell me what you want me to do with my life."

He said, "The first thing I want you to do…IS TO QUIT WORRYING ABOUT WHAT YOU ARE GOING TO DO! You are not a human doing, David, you are a human being. So stop worrying about the 'doing' and just 'be' my child. Abide in me and I will live through you."

Then He said, "Your calling is to be a vessel to honor my Name and to worship me."

Of course it wasn't the practical answer I was hoping for; it was simpler and more profound than that. God's wisdom is like that. It's deep and mysterious, and yet somehow accessible and real, all at the same time.

From that memorable encounter, I "received" a song:

"Vessel Of Worship"

Lord make me Yours
Set me apart
Not just with most
But with all of my heart

85.

Weaned from the world, fearless to follow
Your will as my joy
Your grief as my sorrow, make me a

Vessel of worship, a vessel of praise
A vessel to honor You all of my days
Take my life and my song
Lord I long to belong to You
Gladly resign
Heart body and mind
As a vessel of honor
A vessel of praise
A vessel of worship to You

Let me hear Your Voice and live
See Your Face and die
Lord lead me to the Rock
So much higher than I
To dwell in Your Glory
See the Face of Your Son
O the joy I'm a child
Of the Holy One, I'm a

Vessel of worship, a vessel of praise
A vessel to honor You all of my days
Take my life and my song
Lord I long to belong to You
Gladly resign
Heart body and mind
As vessel of honor
A vessel of praise
A vessel of worship to You

David Baroni / Bridge Building Music/ BMI/CCLI

86.

I had hoped for a faxed itinerary from God. Instead I was given an invitation to enter an eternal adventure of intimacy with Christ. The choice was mine. I could keep living dutifully, serving God in my own strength, surviving and trying my best (and in vain) to keep my world "safe;" or I could trust the One Who called me, like Peter, to step out of the boat, to color outside the lines, to morph from my black and white existence and learn how to live in color.

Growing up on Oriole Terrace in Natchez, we were one of the last families I knew to keep our old black and white TV. I remember when my friend across the street invited me over to see his family's brand new color television. It was a wonderful, exciting world. The reds, the blues, the greens…

Even golf looked glamorous and vibrant on that TV set (I have since learned to love golf, playing it and watching it, but back then it seemed about as exciting as watching paint dry).

The difference between religiosity - keeping the rules, being like everybody else, trying to earn God's love - and having a real relationship with God, with one's self, with others and with God's world, is like the difference between merely existing and really living. I want to live in color.

Spectravision.

Panavision.

DLP with Surround Sound.

William Wallace said, "Every man dies, not every man really lives."

Sadly, I think in some respects American Christians have deserved our reputation as grim-faced, angry people who loudly decry what we are against and rarely let people know what we are for. We seem to fear people who disagree with us; indeed sometimes we seem to fear life itself! Our God is not petty; He is not afraid. He is a whole lot bigger and more generous than I used to believe.

Jazz and Grace

There are a lot of reasons that I love jazz improvisation. To me jazz is a wonderful metaphor of the way to live. In most jazz compositions there is a form. The song starts with the "intro." Like an overture in a musical, the intro can hint of melodies and rhythms to come, whetting the appetite of both player and listener. Then there is the verse melody. Following that is the "B" section, which can be compared to a chorus. After playing through the tune a time or two, the real fun begins.

Musicians begin to solo, playing improvised melodies over the chord changes of the tune. This interaction involves many dynamics. The musicians must listen to each other and make room for the soloist by playing less and not as loudly.

There must be deference between the players, humility if you will. Musicians that flow together well are demonstrating one of the Apostle Paul's admonitions to "prefer one another." With good jazz musicians there is a blend of skill, musical knowledge, a sense of community, and plenty of room for spontaneous creativity.

Even the audience can be part of the music by responding with applause, encouraging shouts, or rapt attention when the music gets soft and subtle. It's kind of like the African American church services my mother took me to when I was a boy. Again, jazz music does have a form, but the form of the song is not the focal point, the music itself is.

As jazz music grew in popularity, some musicians, like trumpeter Miles Davis, came to advocate a kind of music that eschewed form of any kind. It was inevitable that the intoxicating freedom of jazz music would lead to this kind of musical experimentation (and not all of that was unproductive); however, the end result of much of this "free jazz" seemed more like musical anarchy and a cacophony of selfishness than the sound of freedom.

I think that is why some of us fear grace. We mistakenly believe that grace will lead to the appearance of freedom without any form, new wine that is wasted on the ground because there is no wineskin.

One author wisely suggests that when grace is preached, if there is no fear that some will misinterpret the message of grace as license to do whatever they want, then the preacher has not adequately presented grace.

To have true adventure is to sometimes take risks. Indeed to live, to love sometimes involves risk.

I would love to tell you that I immediately understood the implications of God's answer to me that day on the road in Wichita, but, of course that was not the case. I do see, however, that that encounter was a watershed event in my life as the message of God's grace began to break through to me.

All of my life has been lived in the tension between wanting to be a "good boy," safely playing by the rules, being dutiful, loyal and dependable; and the hunger I have had to be adventurous, wild and unpredictable, to be "free."

My theological journey has progressed along these same battle lines, along with my music and songwriting, my marriage and family life, indeed, every aspect of my life. For years I thought that I had to choose between one or the other, between being safe and being free. I am starting to see that real life involves both. Here is a somewhat simplistic analogy of the attempt to have freedom without form:

If a locomotive was a person, I believe that there would be times when that train would longingly look at the meadows, streams, and mountains that lay just outside the confinement of the train tracks.

Perhaps one day that train would leap off of the tracks into what it perceived to be the adventure of freedom. "No tracks to imprison me anymore!" it would cry exultantly.

Of course, we could imagine what would happen next. Without the rails, the "little engine that couldn't" would soon get bogged down in mud or encounter treacherous terrain that it simply could not navigate by itself. The train would then lurch to a stop, or worse, plunge into a ravine.

Equally tragic, though perhaps less easily perceived, would be the train that never lifted its eyes from the tracks to *see* the meadows, the brilliant blue sky, or the mountains and meadows that it passed every day. How sad for this train to one day end up as scrap metal without ever enjoying the journey.

Much of my life I have been more like the second train, but I am learning to *listen* to the music of my life, and not just play or sing it.

-14-
Jazz Preachin'

In his book "Beyond Liberation: The Gospel in the Black American Experience," author Carl F. Ellis shares this wonderful quote, "Jesus was a jazz preacher."

His premise is that instead of filling his head with knowledge and then speaking from rigorously studied texts, Jesus observed life and observed people and spoke extemporaneously about the wonders of ordinary life. His message flowed out of His relationship with His Father and His joy at being alive. What Jesus taught was what He lived, and the message itself was a living thing, like a song.

I have sung in some strange, wonderful, and exotic locations in my years of traveling all over the United States and in 20 nations. There was the Masonic Temple with four podiums (one per side), where a church held services in California, and the Young Buddhist Association Gymnasium in Honolulu, Hawaii. I was moved to tears at a men's prison in Hawaii when I heard them lift their strong voices in praise.

I performed in the middle of the parade ground at an army base where the company was commanded to come hear me. I sang and played with a team from the U.S. in Jakarta, Indonesia in an ornate dinner club that seats 3,000. Elvis had once performed there (I didn't see him that night).

Once I was part of a worship conference in St. Petersburg, Russia. 700 people came from all 11 time zones throughout Russia. We met for 3 days in a former communist indoctrination camp on the edge of the Baltic Sea. It was electrifying to see the excited young people packed sardine-like into an auditorium that ideally held 500.

Though normally I don't like outdoor venues, I did enjoy singing at a Sunday morning worship service on the beach outside the Waikiki Hilton in Honolulu.

On my first trip to Nigeria, I was in a massive auditorium with a tin roof. Right before I got up on the platform to sing, the heavens opened and a mighty rainfall pounded on the roof. There were openings in the walls to see the rain as it poured. I couldn't help but think of the Toto song that has the line, "I bless the rains down in Africa."

Nigerians are beautiful, expressive people who like things to be loud. They talk loudly, they sing loudly, they listen to music at a loud volume. In that same service, many in the congregation had whistles (like coaches use) and at a certain time, they all began to blow them at the same time. It was deafening. Then, the pastor blew his whistle... *into the microphone!* Guest or not, I put tissue in my ears.

Just outside of Lagos in Nigeria, there is a massive campground that is the venue for a monthly Friday night all night praise and preaching meeting. My friend Wale Adenuga from Lagos invited me to sing and play there as part of my tour of Nigeria. I joined with him and his music team, Fountain of Praise, as we braved the crazy Lagos traffic and made our way out to the campground.

When we arrived early in the evening on that Friday, many of the people had yet to arrive. There were "only" about 500,000 people there as we sang! I am told that the crowd is routinely one million people.

I have never seen so many people in one place. There was row upon row of chairs as far as the eye could see, huge video monitors and speakers placed everywhere. The sea of beautiful people, their colorful costumes, and their exuberance was breathtaking.

As memorable as that experience was, some of the most fulfilling moments I've had were in smaller auditoriums and churches. There is something about being with a smaller group of people that fosters an intimacy and a connection that is rarely duplicated in larger settings.

And then there are those times when I am singing and playing for an audience of One.

Winnipeg

There have been a few books that have been pivotal in my growth as a Believer. One of them is "There Were Two Trees in The Garden" by Rick Joyner, a powerful treatise on the difference between serving God in our own strength (eating of the tree of the knowledge of good and evil) and letting Christ *be* our life (eating of the Tree of Life).

Another book that impacted me deeply is "The Saving Life of Christ" by Major Ian W. Thomas.

These books helped me immensely to begin to see my life in Christ as a Divine Romance, the Great Adventure, reminding me that I can live from the inside out instead of a dutiful, plodding, self-sufficient existence.

I had yet to reconcile the jazz/ freestyle basketball/ spontaneous approach to life and music of my past with the demands of packaging and presentation that the music and concert business (and even the western church) seemed to demand. I was in the process of coming into freedom from legalism and my own self-effort.

I had always tried to incorporate some "space" in my concerts to have some free-flowing music. I didn't plan every little detail or even every song, but basically I knew what was going to happen most of the evening.

Then I went to Winnipeg.

While I was in Canada, I discovered and read a couple of books by Dr. LaMar Boschman, a teacher and pioneer in the area of praise and worship music. One of the books was "The Rebirth of Music" which contained many biblical references to the purposes of God for music. The other book was called "The Prophetic Song."

In that book, Boschman mentioned three categories of song in the Bible. There are songs *about* God, songs *to* God, and the third category, which intrigued me: *God* singing! Some theologians believe that God not only spoke the universe into being, He *sung* it.

The idea I was starting to understand is that God sometimes sings to His people *through* His people.

As I read the book, I thought about the times in concerts that I would sense that the Lord wanted to sing a fresh, spontaneously inspired song to the congregation through me.

One such time was in Biloxi, Mississippi, when I told the congregation that I felt that the Lord wanted me to "go out on a limb" and sing a spontaneous song. I did just that (I don't remember what I sang, probably something simple and safe like "I love you my children"), and afterward someone came up to me and told me that he felt like the Lord wanted to tell me that I *was* out on a limb and that "they were going to get shorter."

With the book I had just read and those thoughts fresh in my mind, I walked across the yard from where I was staying into the church auditorium.

There was nobody around, it was the middle of a weekday and the pastor, Jeff Hunt, who was hosting my time in Winnipeg was running some errands.

One of my favorite things to do is play the piano all by myself. There in that empty auditorium I sat at the piano and for the next 45 minutes I played and sang songs I had never played or even heard before!

I was singing a new song that I believe was inspired by the Holy Spirit. I "happened to" record the whole encounter on a small cassette recorder.

I knew that I had had a special time in the Presence of the Lord, but I didn't realize just how significant the encounter was until I was driving down the road in Mississippi about two months later.

Even though I was running a little late to get to my concert (I was a typical man who didn't stop to ask directions), I found the cassette tape that I had recorded in Winnipeg and listened to it for the very first time. I was stunned to hear God Himself singing to me through my voice on the tape. The words and music of that special time in Canada in 1990 came alive to me and touched my heart in such a profound way that I have not been the same since.

Here is an excerpt from that incredible afternoon:

"The Song of the Lord"

So you think you've seen My glory
You think you've seen My power
You haven't seen...
See what I'm about to do this hour

Take all My vessels of clay
Breathe My life within them
Place My Spirit in them
Taking them out of their own ways
While they stand before Me
Hear My orders- feel My heart
They aren't worried about what people say
They are dead to this world and the approval of men
They have only one desire- that's to glorify Me
Will you be one of them my child
I ask you today… join Me

Lay your life down, lay it down
Lay your past; lay your future too.
Lay all your pride and your fear and your worry
And I will melt it away as the morning dew
And I will take you my child
I will love you my son
Do not fear but trust me
Do not count it strange what I will do with you
Throw your plans away
Grow and walk in my ways
I will flow through you
I will be your life
You will see My Life and My Glory manifested

If you enter My gates with thanksgiving
And enter My courts with praise
You will never have to leave again
For I am your dwelling place
I will go with you through the valley
On the mountaintop so high
I have put My words and My life within you
Ever lift Me, lift Me high

I'll go with you through the valley
Through the laughter and the pain
I will go with you through the desert
I'll be the pouring rain
I will keep your feet from shaking
When everything around you looks dim
I am your Rock in a fearful land
I am my child and I'll always be here

You're my child- don't try to avoid
The suffering you will see
For in the midst of those trials
You'll more clearly see Me.

And I assure you it's just for a short time
Then your walk will be through
There will be no fleshly limitations
You'll be free to worship Me
From your heart for eternity

Safe here inside Me
You'll live forever
You will never be ashamed
Of Me and My words and My love song

My worlds were starting to come together. What I believe God was speaking to me was a declaration of His steadfast love. I also heard a call, a challenge, to open my heart and my mind, to stop playing it safe and depending on my natural ability to play music, write songs, or move a crowd.

Instead I heard an invitation to launch out into the deep of trusting that He will give me what to sing, play, or say as I listen for His voice. In other words, to give the Holy Spirit time to communicate through me what is on His heart for a particular audience or congregation, and in my daily life.

This was not anything new, though it was new for me. The Quakers of old began their meetings sitting quietly, waiting for someone to be moved upon by the Holy Spirit to speak, pray, or share. I didn't take what I was hearing to that extreme; indeed I still planned a song list most of the time and had an idea beforehand what I would share. However, I was more willing to allow time and room for spontaneous songs, or to throw away my notes if I felt like the Holy Spirit was going in a different direction. It was a bit scary sometimes, but exciting too.

I even staring allowing time for instrumental improvisation (or "flowing in the Spirit" if you prefer that term). Once I was in Athens, Greece in a meeting that had people from about 22 different language groups. We had translators (in little booths like the United Nations) for only three or four languages.

As I was singing and speaking, I became frustrated with the language barriers. Then I got inspired. I told the people that I was going to ask the Lord to speak to them in their language through the music that I would play.

I let them know that this would be a spontaneous song, that I didn't know what I was going to play but that I would trust the Lord for grace. I also encouraged them to close their eyes and open their hearts.

After praying for God to use my fingers to play and use the music to help the people hear His voice, I began. The room became silent, then the Presence of the Lord began to be experienced in an almost tangible way. His peace filled the room; some people began to quietly weep. I played for about 6 or 7 minutes and then we continued on with the concert.

Afterward, several people came up to me and through a translator told me that they had seen visions or heard God's voice through the music and were greatly moved. Since that time, I have tried to be sensitive to do spontaneous instrumental songs when it seemed to be appropriate.

This experience was the inspiration for launching my FingerPaintings solo piano series of recordings. I will go into a studio, sit down at the piano and just play and record as I am spontaneously inspired. Then the sound engineer and I will choose the best 45 minutes or so and release that as a solo piano CD. These recordings have been remarkably well-received.

Sometimes the words that say it best are not words at all.

-15-
Loss and Laughter

Rita got the call one evening in our first year of marriage. Her grandmother, Ida Clarissa Robinson of Totz, Kentucky, had passed away after struggling with cancer for a few years. We set out that night for the long drive into the coal mining mountains of eastern Kentucky.

Rita had been particularly impacted by her maternal grandmother, who was a God-fearing, tough, capable mountain woman who had raised 7 children by herself after her husband ran away from the marriage and from the mountains. When Rita would stay with her grandma, the attention and care she received helped to lessen the pain caused, felt and inflicted upon by her immediate family.

This was the first time in our young marriage that we were confronted with grief. I tried to be loving and supportive but I still remember how helpless I felt in the presence of Rita's sadness. Being a man, I wanted to "fix it" and I couldn't. I have since learned that sometimes just being there, listening and caring is enough.

After winding through the mountains, sometimes having to slow to 15 miles per hour to make the hairpin turns; we arrived at Rita's aunt Willa's home at around 11:00 P:M.

I made the mistake of indulging in a large portion of Uncle Reb's delicious spaghetti. After talking with relatives and eating, Rita and I made our way to the mobile home perched on the side of the mountain, which was to be our lodging for the next few days. Though I was exhausted from the trip I could not sleep. My emotions, thoughts, and the spaghetti were tumbling around inside of me.

At around 2:30 in the morning I heard a blood-curdling bellow from deep in the woods next to the trailer. Visions of Bigfoot on a rampage danced through my addled brain. Rita heard it too. We prayed for protection. We heard the deep throated growl again. Was it a huge bear; A monster? After hearing the dreadful, alien cry yet again we waited in the stifling summer silence. I eventually drifted off to sleep.

The next day we related our nocturnal adventure to the family. Instead of sympathy, they howled with laughter. We had heard a cow in heat and the husbandly ministration of a very grateful bull!

A Goodbye

In early 1985 on a visit to my boyhood home in Natchez, my mother called Rita and me out to the front porch that overlooked the railroad tracks and the stately Stanton Hall mansion.

My mother looked at us teary-eyed and said: "Six months". I didn't understand what she meant at first, but then she told us that she had cancer and that the doctors' had given her six months to live.

She actually lived longer than six months, finally succumbing to the disease in March of 1986.

I remember the last time I saw my mother, one week before she died. I had driven back to Natchez from Nashville.

I went by myself because Rita was pregnant (she eventually miscarried) and Bethany was just a baby. Because of my concert schedule I had to leave Nashville late and drove all night. I had wanted to spare my young family the grueling trip.

And…I went alone because I just needed to.

In my narrow view at the time of the grace of God, I wanted some assurance from my mother of her salvation. Looking back now, I wish I hadn't been so uptight, but that's where I was at the time, concerned for my mother's soul.

As I sat on her bed and looked at her emaciated face and form, I asked her: "Mama, have you asked Jesus into your heart?" She replied in her feisty, intelligent way: "David, if you are asking me if I have had an emotional, cathartic experience like you did, the answer is no I have not. If you are asking me if I have asked Jesus to forgive me, the answer is yes, every day, for the sins I know I have committed, for and even for the ones I haven't known about."

That was my mama!

On that lonely trip from Nashville to Natchez, one week before my mother passed away, as I was driving into Adams County, the county of my birth, I was listening to a song by Twila Paris called "Lamb of God". It was about four in the morning and the floodgates opened. My tears and my grief came pouring out. I did a lot of my grieving before she died.

My brother Neil seemed to take Mama's death the hardest. His advocate, his confidant, his hero had died. He was not doing well emotionally, and understandably so. Our family and friends grieved just to see his grief.

Neil wanted to give the eulogy. Knowing that he would probably not be able to be rational in that situation, my brother Philip wisely suggested that Neil play the organ instead.

In an earlier chapter I told about singing at my mom's funeral. I didn't tell you however, about Neil's organ solo.

In the cavernous St. Mary's Cathedral, the choir and organ loft is in the rear of the sanctuary and was accessed by a narrow corkscrew stairway. The funeral congregation faces the front, where the priest and other leaders of the service hold forth.

The church was packed. Everything was going pretty smoothly, except for the priest accidentally whacking my mother's casket with the censer of incense. I sang my songs from up in the choir loft. Neil was also in the choir loft and Philip was with Neil, waiting to help him if he had a breakdown.

Neil was calm, like the eye of a hurricane. Then it was time for his organ solo. He had chosen to play one of my mother's favorite songs: "Amazing Grace".

Neil walked to the organ, then unknowingly (or knowingly!) *stepped on the bass pedals* as he found his seat. The dissonant, thunderous, disjointed bass notes that rang out from his feet were the first clue that this rendition of Amazing Grace was not going to be typical.

Then he started playing.

This brilliant musician was playing discordant, child-like, horror movie style music at my mama's funeral. He was out of it, beside himself with grief and he had not taken his depression medication. My sister Mary Jane, seated downstairs in the sanctuary next to my wife said, "Tell me that's not Neil." Of course without even looking around, she knew that it was.

He did manage to play a couple of bars of a jazzy Amazing Grace, then, mercifully, it was over.

The family has laughed many times over that organ solo.

Neil died in 2006 after spending his last few months in a nursing home in his beloved Natchez, playing piano for the patients and elderly friends that he met there. At his funeral I sang "He is Here"; a song that I had also sung at my mother's funeral:

He's the One Who made the heavens

Spoke the stars into the sky

He's the One Who puts the sparkle

In a baby's eyes

You can hear Him in the sweetness

Of a mother's lullaby

Yet so marvelous it is to realize

That He's right here

He is here let's celebrate the presence of the Lord

He is here, the Holy One, Oh let Him be adored

He is here, to worship Him is such a sweet reward

He is here in our midst

He is here
(David Baroni/ Niles Borop/ NB Music/ Soldier of the Light Music/BMI)

I also played and sang a newer song, one that made me think about my brother almost every time I ever sang it. It is a song called "Within the Heart of God".

"Within the Heart of God"
David Baroni /2003 Kingdomsongs /BMI

There is a Rock, a rest for stumbling feet
A shelter for the wandering
There is a place where sin and mercy meet
Within the Heart of God

There is a Peace to heal the troubled mind
A silence from the thundering
There is a hope the hopeless soul can find
Within the Heart of God

O Love that chases fear away
And Strength to run and win the race
The heart will find its resting place
Within the Heart of God

He was sad, funny, poignant, disconnected, sometimes shocking. A genius, a father, a brother, a friend, a teacher; that was Neil. That was my brother.

-16-
Trouble in Paradise

After Charity and Celeste were born, we tried to continue traveling together as a family, but after about five months, we finally realized that it was just too taxing on Rita and everyone else to keep up a road schedule.

So Rita stayed at home, busy with a toddler and infant twins. I traveled and sang, and traveled some more. The year that the twins were born was one of my busiest years, which was great financially but not so good for my family in other ways.

I will never forget driving away our home on Stoney Brook Circle in Antioch to go to the airport with Bethany, Charity and Celeste leaning on to the front door crying because they didn't want Daddy to leave again.

Somehow we survived those first few years when our children were very young and required so much attention. I think most of the time Rita and I both were on automatic pilot-in survival mode.

In the early 90's (not long after the special "God-Encounter" I had in Canada), I received an invitation to be on staff as a worship pastor at a fairly large church in Nashville. We had started attending this particular church after leaving the denomination we had been a part of for eleven years.

It was no easy thing to leave the Woodbine church. Our children had been dedicated there. I worked with several of the men of that church for years in the concrete construction business. This small community of people was our second family. We were at each other's children's births. We had a lot of fun and fellowship together over those eleven years. These were good, salt-of -the-earth people.

However, we had heard and seen some things that we felt were from the Lord that were different from the accepted doctrinal view that most of those folks had, and we finally realized that if we were going to keep growing spiritually we had to leave that church- knowing that some of our friends would consider our leaving as tantamount to leaving God.

Right after we made our decision, Rita and I had a timely trip to Alaska to sing in Anchorage and Fairbanks and Wasilla, a small town about an hour from Anchorage.

While we were there our hosts were Larry and Janet Biggers. Larry had been a pastor in Hawaii when we took our first trip over there to be in concerts that he arranged. He and his family had been missionaries in Samoa, moved to Hawaii where we met them, and now were living in Alaska.

Larry and Janet have always been generous in spirit and good listeners so when we got off the plane I began to tell them the whole story of our exodus from our former local church. They were part of the same denomination and understood a lot about our circumstances. After I told them the whole story, I wondered if I had talked too much. I went to sleep with a lot of anxiety.

When I woke up the next morning, the first thing I was aware of was how peaceful I felt. My anxiety, my questions were dissolved in the Presence of the Lord. Later, in Larry's office, I wrote this song:

Captured by Your Presence Lord
In this holy place
All my questions fade away
In Your sweet embrace

When we arrived back in Nashville I made another decision. Though being a worship pastor was not something I necessarily aspired to, (or felt qualified for,) it seemed like a good move for me to accept the position at Bethel Chapel. Rita loves to quote cosmetic legend Mary Kay: "God doesn't necessarily call the qualified, he qualifies the called."

Though it was a challenge to be on staff at a local church, I enjoyed working with the choir and worship team and other staff members. Our church recorded three "live" CDs featuring some of my songs. Rita and I were growing spiritually. Our theology was receiving a much needed major overhaul and most importantly, I was at home with my wife and children.

This was a new paradigm for me and Rita. As difficult as my travel schedule had been for us in some ways, it was a routine that we had adjusted to and made the best of. In the past, if Rita and I got in some kind of disagreement, I would just bide my time until the weekend, then I would get out of Dodge. (We didn't know at the time conflict could be a healthy part of our relationship.)

I would go to some convention or concert where I was usually the center of attention, I would be told how wonderful I was, get paid, and return home.

In the meantime, Rita would have had time to process whatever the issue was, or be so busy taking care of our children that she wouldn't have time to think about it. We would have missed each other too, so when I came home we would have a day or so of "re-entry", then get on with our lives and marriage, leaving the root conflicts not dealt with. With my new position however, I couldn't just leave when things got tough.

In what had become a rare travel date, Rita and I took a trip to Sonora, California, to sing and to be with our friends Craig and Diane Andrus. They had moved from the L.A. area close to breathtaking Yosemite National Park.

We had a great time with the Andrus family, but Rita and I were not getting along very well with each other. What we had intended as a nice vacation for just the two of us became a tense standoff that had us both on the defensive with each other.

The night we returned from our unhappy getaway, as we were preparing for bed Rita said, "We need to have a talk soon." I replied uncharacteristically: "How about right now?" (Usually I would have brushed off her comment and hoped she would forget about it but I had a feeling that this was serious.)

We sat at the kitchen table in our home on Stoney Brook and Rita said: "I haven't been happy in these twelve years of marriage." As stunned as I was to hear that, I was even more surprised with what I heard myself say: "Neither have I."

It was a long night.

We had already scheduled an appointment with a marriage counselor to deal with some problems in our relationship. When the day for our session arrived and we spoke with the psychologist, I was not prepared for her assessment:
"You both have some major issues here and you need more help than I can give you by myself. I am calling in my husband (also a trained psychologist) to meet with us as well. We are talking about weekly intense work here for an extended period of time."

My jaw dropped open. I couldn't believe it! I had naively thought that one or two sessions and Rita would get all straightened out! (Yes I am joking, but I am ashamed to admit that that wasn't very far away from the way I perceived things, which was, of course, a major part of our problem!)

After one of our first sessions, our "homework" was to go see a funny movie and laugh.

Rita and I had been terminally serious from the beginning of our life together. We both grew up in intense family situations - she with her dad's alcoholism and the fighting between her mom and dad; me with the civil rights struggle, my mother's rage and fear and Neil's mental illness.

Add to that the apocalyptic seriousness of the church we had been a part of, and the financial pressures of raising children on an income that depended largely on unpredictable sales and "love offerings", and it is no wonder that we were way too serious.

Listening closely to our marriage coaches, we worked hard, prayed hard, loved each other and tried to follow our counselors' words of wisdom. After about one year, this couple who had become marriage savers, told us that we had done well, and they released us with their blessing.

Life was good, our marriage was stronger and we communicated much better. Our daughters were doing well in school, and even though I wasn't traveling, my music was going further than ever.

Integrity Music

It had been a dream of mine to write for Integrity Music, a company that sprung up in the 80's that had an emphasis on recording "live" praise and worship music. From the moment I heard some of those early recordings I wanted to be an Integrity songwriter and worship leader.

One of my predecessors at Bethel, John Chisum, had moved down to Mobile Alabama to be the director of Song Development at Integrity. John and I and our mutual friend George Searcy, who co-led worship with John, had written songs together while they were still in Nashville (George moved to Louisiana to return to seminary).

John became an advocate for me and the executives at Integrity heard and liked my songs. They offered me a three year exclusive songwriting contract and I accepted.

That three years became six and people like Alvin Slaughter, (whom I had met in New York when he was with the Brooklyn Tabernacle Choir), Ron Kenoly, Sheila Walsh, Don Moen, Paul Wilbur and others recorded my songs.

I also got to sing and record some of my songs as part of the Acoustic Worship Songwriter Series along with other songwriters like Paul Baloche, Darrell Evans, Lincoln Brewster, Bob Fitts and Lynn Deshazo who wrote "More Precious Than Silver".

We did those recordings after two different songwriters' retreats, where we hung out, rehearsed each other's songs and laughed and prayed together. It was special to be a part of that group of creative people.

After three years on staff at Bethel, I felt the stirrings of change once again and I resigned to resume my itinerant ministry. In the month after I resigned I was once again on the road without a regular salary. I had become very comfortable with knowing how much I was going to be paid every two weeks and now it was back to love offerings.

LaMar Boschman and I met when he came to teach at a regional Worship Institute in Nashville. He invited me to come on a trip to Singapore with a team from the Worship Institute.

While I was there I told the seven hundred conference attendees in an afternoon session:

"I have always hoped for the right ministry or financial circumstance or a mountaintop encounter with God that would take away my need to ever be concerned about things like finances again. I have wanted to engineer my circumstances so that I would never have to worry again. I am coming to realize that there is no such circumstance or resting place. The only resting place is a person and His name is Jesus, and I believe that God designed things that way so that we would learn to rest in Him and not in our ability to engineer situations to our liking."

Oh I could teach it well, but learning it is a daily, lifelong thing.

On that same trip, after the last night of the conference, a young man approached me. He thanked me for my music and then held out a handkerchief with some rocks in it. He said: "Last night on my way home from the conference the Lord told me to bring these stones tonight and that I was to give them to someone. Tonight he showed me that I was to give them to you."

He went on to say that he had been traveling in Israel one year earlier and had stopped in the valley where David and Goliath had fought. In that valley the Lord spoke to him to pick up five stones. (David had picked up five smooth stones to defeat Goliath.) The Lord didn't tell him what to do with those stones until the last night of our conference. He continued: "Tonight the Lord told me to give these stones to you. He says that you are a David and that He wants you to remember that it's not by might, not by power, but by My Spirit says the Lord."

I still have those stones in a prominent place in my home.

-17-
Off Broadway

Bethany started on the Jr. High girls' basketball team in eighth grade. I volunteered to help out as assistant coach. We enjoyed practicing together and it was a great way to spend daddy-daughter time. Our whole family rarely missed a game.

Halfway through the season the head coach wasn't able to continue, so the board asked me to be the head coach for the rest of the year. I had a good time working with the girls. We ended up winning the Home School National Championship in a yearly tournament in Wichita, KS.

As Charity and Celeste progressed to High School, I also got to coach their basketball team. Like Bethany, the twins were gifted athletes and competitive. The other team's point guard dreaded being double-teamed by the Baroni girls. More times than not, one of them would come up with a steal.

Once we were beating a team by 20 points in the third quarter so I pulled starters Charity and Celeste out of the game in order to not run up the score. The other team scored 8 points fairly quickly and my girls got a bit nervous.

"Dad, put us back in!"

I didn't, and we won the game. But I admit I also got a little nervous for a moment there!

We took many yearly trips to Wichita every spring for the

basketball tournament. Usually we had some other team members with us and the van we traveled in is still a sentimental favorite with my girls and their friends.

So often my life has been adventurous, with a lot of exciting memories of the people I have met and the places I have been. I used to live from conference to conference, from excitement to excitement. Now I realize that real life is in the daily, the routine, the ordinary, wonderful moments like taking my daughters to basketball practice, having coffee with a friend, a long talk about big and little things with my wife. I even enjoy mowing our yard. "Ordinary" life is extraordinary.

The reformers had an expression to live life "Coram Deo", *before the face of God.*
Not just worship services or special occasions, but everyday life is sacred. Martin Luther King Jr. echoed those reformers as he encouraged the street sweeper not to belittle his occupation, but instead, given grace and dignity by God, he should aspire to be the best street sweeper in the world.

The Bishop

I had a concert at a church in Memphis in the early nineties, and Rita went with me on the 3 hour drive from Nashville. The church was predominately African American and after I sang, we enjoyed hearing from the guest speaker; a preacher from West Virginia named T.D. Jakes.

After the meeting, Rita and I went out to eat with Bishop Jakes and his wife Serita. We had a nice meal, traded "war" stories of life in the ministry, and said our farewells.

A few years later, Bishop Jakes had risen to national prominence, was a very visible presence on television, and moved to Dallas to start a church called The Potter's House which now numbers several thousand members.

T.D. Jakes and Tyler Perry had written and produced a play that had a phenomenal run at the Apollo Theater in Harlem in New York and in other theaters around the country. The play was called "Woman, Thou Art Loosed", and left audiences cheering and crying and shouting for more. Good theater is powerful.

One day I got a call from friends Tim and Que English, whom we had met on the road. At this time Que was working at the Potter's House with Bishop Jakes:

"David, Tyler Perry and the Bishop are working on a new play and they are looking for a "white guy who can sing" to be one of the main characters. Bishop Jakes remembers meeting you and hearing you. Would you be open to considering being a part of this new play? Can you come to New York *tomorrow* for an audition?"

I thought about this potential career change. I love the theater. I still vividly remember seeing "Godspell" on Broadway with my parents when I was a child.

After some thought, talking it over with Rita and some prayer, I agreed to audition though I was a bit reluctant because I had had very little acting experience. Oh well, if nothing else, it would be a free trip to The Big Apple.

I arrived at LaGuardia Airport the next day and was taken by limo to the Trump International Hotel bordering Central Park in Manhattan.

With nervous anticipation I took the elevator to the eighth floor suite where the audition was being held. It was good to see Bishop Jakes again. He warmly welcomed me and introduced me to director and playwright Tyler Perry.

After some small talk, they directed me to stand in the space in front of the fireplace and tell them something about myself. I told them that I was the male lead in my senior play in high school, and that I had been featured in a Diadem Records

musical called "The Story". Then they asked me to
sing- acapella.

I took a deep breath, then sang a song I wrote called
"When You Walk Through the Water":

Lord I want to be led by Your Spirit
But sometimes I feel so afraid
Other times like Jacob, I wrestle with you Lord
While my foolish heart tries to have its own way
And even when I think I'm strong Lord
You know I'm weak and frail
That's why I put my trust in You
Then You remind me of this promise that won't fail
I hear You say:

"When you walk through the water
I will be with you
And the river will not overflow you, though you
Walk through the water
I will be with you
Through the flood or flame
You won't be burned or drowned
I'm the God Who lifts You up
And I'll never let you down"

(David Baroni/ Bridgebuilding Music/ BMI)

When I sing, I am free. I can be myself.

Paradoxically, I am not self-conscious; I am conscious
that the song is bigger than me.

My mother and father told me that when I was a boy in
Mississippi I woke up singing. I have always had a song. I
loved the poem "I Know Why the Caged Bird Sings" by Maya
Angelou:

115.

The caged bird sings not because it has an answer, but because it has a song.

Well, that day in the Trump International Hotel I sang from my heart. The Bishop and Tyler Perry must have liked what they heard because they invited me to be a part of the play!

My flight was scheduled to leave at 6 P: M that day, so I declined an invitation from Bishop Jakes to go to the Apollo Theater and see "Woman Thou Art Loosed." He said they would change my flight, yet I declined again.

This is why I said no:

In 1998 we got a call from Rita's mother. She was diagnosed with colon cancer. The prognosis was not good. She died in May of 1999.

When Rita heard that her mother was dying, something died in Rita. It was the dream of having a good relationship with her mom. My mother-in-law had been deeply wounded by life, by abuse in the Kentucky mountains, and by a husband that put alcohol and partying before his wife and children. She was also imprisoned by a fear-based, narrow view of God.

Though in some ways Charlene had done the best she could to keep her family together- she was a hard worker and could be very generous at times- she didn't know how to affirm and nurture her daughter Rita.

Much of the time her words were cutting and humiliating. I guess she couldn't give what she didn't have.

Rita, on the other hand, was a wonderful mother to our daughters. We were very careful about the words we spoke in our children's hearing and tried to be encouraging.

Rita had done some good work with our counselors to process some of her childhood "stuff". She was hopeful that there could be a good relationship with her mother eventually. Then Charlene got sick.

As I said, when that happened, Rita got heartsick. She began to be angry; at her mother, at me, at life, at God. She also questioned whether or not she wanted to stay married. Despite the progress of our earlier counseling, I had regressed to living on auto-pilot again. I was not physically present due to my travel schedule; and when I was around, I was not emotionally available either. Our marriage was in trouble. We needed help.

We found ourselves back at the counselors' office- the husband and wife team that had released us seven years earlier.

"What happened?" I groaned. "How come we're back here again?"

They explained that we had gone as deep as we could go in the healing process some seven years earlier but that this time we were going to go all the way to the roots of our issues, and that if we would cooperate with God, however painful the healing process would be, He would do a deeper, more thorough work in each of us individually and in our marriage.

I was scared. Rita didn't want to be married and there was nothing I could do about it. When I would admit it I wasn't so sure I wanted to be married either.

Somehow we hung in there and began the slow, painful process of healing and learning how to be individuals as well as a couple.

When we got married, I thought that me as an individual would rightly cease to exist; it was a woeful misinterpretation of the scripture: "And the two shall become one flesh".

One of the things I learned through this round of counseling was that in every marriage there are three entities: The man, the woman, and the "coupleship".

One of my main problems is that I had idolized Rita. I had

looked to her to make me whole, to fill up the wounds in my life that abuse in my childhood and an emotionally absent mother had caused.

Ultimately of course, only God can heal those wounds and fill those places in our hearts. I was putting way too much pressure on Rita to meet needs she wasn't capable of, or even supposed to meet. After all, she wasn't my Savior.

For her part, perhaps she wanted me to be the handsome prince on the white horse that was her rescuer, her escape from the craziness and pain of her own childhood. I didn't know how to fill that role; I was not qualified to be her Savior either.

We were given no pre-marital instructions and we were not prepared for the give-and-take and the adjustments that are inevitable in a successful marriage. As Rita puts it, when we were first married it was as if we were instructed to go into a field and build a house together. We had no blueprints, no tools, and no clue as to how to go about the task; so pretty soon we just picked up some rocks and started throwing them at each other!

In this difficult season, this dark night of the soul, we coped as best we could. We tried to avoid each other, we prayed, we cried, we paid a lot of money for individual and marriage counseling, we gave up, we fought, we loved each other, we blamed each other, we waited, we hoped, we gave up again, we worked, we felt pain, we felt numb, we learned how to talk, to disagree and it not be the end of the world.

I started appreciating the small pleasures in life; the smell of coffee in the morning, a smile from my daughter, and a walk in our neighborhood in beautiful, hilly Middle Tennessee with autumn in the air.

A real key for me was having some guy friends to talk to like my brother Philip and my friend Mike Pugh. I needed men in my life that I could be totally honest and safe with.

Over time, (more time than I liked), Rita and I also learned to listen to each other, to really listen. We learned how to forgive one another and not expect perfection out of ourselves, each other or our children. (Forgive us, girls).

Most importantly, I learned how to begin loving and accepting myself and I started seeing just how big and good God is- that I can call Him Father.

I will never forget the day one of our counselors told us that we had been "dis-illusioned." The term that had a negative connotation to me, was in this case actually a very positive one.

We were lovingly and firmly forced to let go of our illusions of what life is, what marriage is, so that we could begin to live in reality.

Our marriage died and a new marriage was born. It took much longer than I would have chosen, but God's painful mercy was teaching us about ourselves in the process. One difficult phrase that I have learned to love that I heard many times is: "Trust the process".

Now I can say thankfully, not smugly, that Rita and I are best friends; we know how to fight fair now, and make up! Our marriage has not only survived, it is thriving- (and for a longer while than I care to remember, the survival of our marriage was not guaranteed.) It was humbling to be told by more than one psychologist that the survival of our relationship is a "miracle", but we will take the miracle!

Meanwhile, Back in New York City…"

So we were in the middle of our struggles when I went on the audition. When Bishop Jakes invited me to go to the Apollo I was frankly not thinking too clearly, I was preoccupied with my home life. I thought it would be best to get on home- but God had other plans.

When the limo dropped me off back at the LaGuardia airport, I rushed inside the terminal to find out that most flights had been canceled because of stormy weather- including all flights to Nashville!

I called the Jakes' people and they sent a ride for me that brought me to the legendary Apollo Theater in Harlem.

The atmosphere for the play was electric. I was privileged to sit in the V.I.P. box with Bishop Jakes and his wife. "Woman Thou Art Loosed" was a powerful musical and the band and actors were amazing. It was a wonderful, powerful, accessible presentation of the Love of God and the people responded extravagantly. We had "church" at the Apollo.

I will never forget sitting in a barbecue rib restaurant at 2 in the morning in Harlem with the entourage from the play that I was to be a part of. We were eating delicious food, celebrating the wonderful night at the Apollo, reading lines from the new play- I could see how some would be hooked on the Broadway life!

We started rehearsals a few weeks later in Dallas. Tyler Perry was the co-author and director of the play which had the provocative title: "Behind Closed Doors."

This was a story of betrayal and redemption, an attempt to reach out to those people who wouldn't necessarily darken the door of a church by means of a musical.

I played the role of an airline pilot with an ill wife. We worked hard on the play, I was enjoying this new chapter in my life, yet I missed being home.

Tyler worked hard and was patient with me; however we came to the conclusion that though my singing was working well, I was not much of an actor. One day during rehearsal he said: "take ten everybody- David you stay here for a minute."

This genius director, who has since become wildly successful with his "Diary of a Mad Black Woman" and television and movie projects, was gracious, yet to the point:

"We have a problem here, David. Your understudy is doing better than you are. What should I do?"

He went on to tell me that I could go on the road with the play and be an understudy, but that he didn't want me to have to endure the ridicule of trying to perform in the play before I was ready- and that there was not enough time for me to get up to speed as an actor. He said that theater audiences, particularly black audiences, could be unmerciful.

Sensing that he was trying to let me down as gently as possible, I quickly assured him that I had a "life" and a calling musically and that it wouldn't be necessary for me to continue with the play. I thanked him for the experience. I even wrote a song that they eventually used in the play.

Tyler told me that if they ever needed somebody to play Farmer Ed, they would be sure to call me. (I must have been really bad!) He told me he was serious about that so Tyler, I'll wait.

I was disappointed, of course, and I even cried a little when I called Rita with the news, but looking back, had I done the play, I would have been on the road for my daughter Bethany's entire senior year in High School. Also, our marriage really needed the attention that we were able to give it.

I appreciate Bishop Jakes and the way he and his staff handled the whole thing- he even invited me to be on an international television program that he hosted. Rita and I were invited to attend the premier of the play in Atlanta, all expenses paid, where she got to meet some of the cast members I had worked with.

So I didn't get to be on Broadway, but I am still happily married and I still have a life and a song!

-18-
Reel to Real

It is intriguing and amazing to me to see how recording technology has changed in my lifetime. When I first started listening to music, most recordings were made by setting up one or two microphones in a big sound studio and having everyone play and sing "live". There was mono recording, then came stereo.

Listening to old Beatle records, the drums and other instruments would be on the left speaker, the vocals and maybe a guitar solo or harmonica would be on right speaker and it was interesting to fade from left to right.

When I was about 14 years old, I start experimenting with "sound on sound" or as it came to be known, overdubbing.

Since I didn't have a lot of recording equipment, (and the technology was in its infancy anyway), I would record piano and lead vocal on a reel to reel tape recorder I borrowed from my brother Neil. Then I would play the reel to reel recording back and play a bass part and a harmony vocal- all going into a Radio Shack cassette tape recorder. I got a lot of tape hiss, but the parts were still distinguishable.

Recording this way; utilizing the technology that was

available, (primitive though it was), helped me in a number of ways. While I played one instrument I would think of the other instruments that I would add, I learned to harmonize vocally by singing along with "myself", and it gave me a hunger to be more creative as a songwriter and musician.

In the 60's and 70's recording techniques had progressed to the point that studios had at least 16 tracks that could be recorded at different times, one track built on another. This process was called overdubbing. Most studios quickly added 8 more to make 24 tracks recorded on 2 inch wide Ampeg recording tape.

I was impressed with musician/ songwriters like Todd Rundgren and Stevie Wonder who often would play every instrument and sing all the parts on their projects. I used whatever tools were at my disposal to emulate them and tap into my musical creativity.

Though some wish that they were born in another age, perhaps at the time of Christ walking with His disciples or in the Renaissance period, I am convinced that I was born at just the right time.

I remember when the Fender Rhodes electric piano was produced. It had a cooler, jazzier sound than the rather dark and limited Wurlitzer electric piano that preceded it (which has now come back into vogue). It was more portable than a piano or B-3 organ and a lot of jazz and pop piano players including my brother Neil added the Rhodes to their collection.

I previously mentioned that I owned a "portable" electric piano called the Yamaha CP-70 Electric Grand. It actually had strings and hammers, (unlike the Rhodes, which had tines), and sounded more like a real piano. Billy Joel, Ray Charles and others helped make that keyboard popular for a while.

One drawback to the CP-70, (besides the fact that it took

123.

two people to move it), was that it had to be tuned often. I learned how to tune it, but I wasn't very patient and didn't do it very well. I think the keyboard that started the synthesizer revolution in a big way was the Yamaha DX-7 that came around in the early 1980s. That keyboard was lightweight and versatile. It had a lot of pre-set sounds that could be modified and stored in the instrument. However, the feature that set it apart from earlier keyboards was one that rocked my world. It had MIDI: **M**usical **I**nstrument **D**igital **I**nterface.

In other words, if I hooked up a DX-7 to other instruments, what I played on one keyboard would be transmitted via MIDI to the other keyboard that was set to a different sound.

Soon, digital recording and technology- recording music into computers that was stored as digital information- began to revolutionize the music industry.

Now days, I can record a song demo into my computer, then email the song instantly to Singapore where a friend could hear a song mere moments after I finished writing and recording it.

With the advent and proliferation of the internet, now I can upload songs to my web-site and literally 24 hours a day people who have internet access from all around the world can hear my music!

Some musical groups have started electronically- or should I say cybernetically. The musicians met in cyber-space, swapped instrumental tracks, each adding their own specialty sounds and formed a band, selling downloads of their music before they ever met in person!

A popular and wonderfully gifted Nashville session guitarist, David Cleveland who has played on some of my projects, tells me of times when he will be at a "live" rehearsal and when there is a lunch break, he will play guitar into his computer and then email the guitar tracks – top quality, no sound loss- to a producer in a studio without ever having to leave the rehearsal!

Now some readers are no doubt thinking: "Cool!" Others are probably thinking, "How horrible- we've replaced the need for human interaction!"

Of course there are pros and cons to technological innovations and if one hides behind a computer all day without "interfacing" with real human beings that is certainly not healthy. My point in bringing up the advances in musical and recording technology is that someone with something to say can say it to a lot of people without having to have big bucks to go into a high-end recording studio, (which still have an important place in the production of music), or be on a record label.

The exciting thing for me is that I have a passion to communicate and a passion to create. I love to write and record music (instrumental and vocal) and modern technology affords me the opportunity to do just that relatively inexpensively.

Despite all that I have just described, I am not a "techno-head." I still have enough of the mindset of the jazz purist to keep bringing me back to what is most important, and that is, of course, the music itself- the song.

A well-produced, expensively recorded, poorly written song is just a nice sounding bad song after all. I want to write songs that mean something to the listener, that encourage and inspire them. I hope my songs communicate and connect with people, maybe help teach something, and make the listener aware of the peace and the Presence of God.

By many measures, I have had success in the music business- the fact that I have been doing this music thing full time for so long is one testament of my success. In the music world, as in life, it is difficult not to fall prey to the joy-sapping, gratitude-robbing spirit of comparison.

There is always someone who can play or sing better, who writes better songs or who has more visibility, more money. One night I had a whisper from my Creator that helped me to put things back in perspective.

Several years ago when the girls were small, we were traveling in our van to yet another church in Alabama. It was late at night and Rita and the girls were asleep. I started thinking about the fact that I didn't have a big recording contract, that others who had started at the same time I did were, at least outwardly, much more successful than I perceived myself to be.

Hoping that maybe God wouldn't notice my jealousy, I couched my complaint in spiritual sounding terms:

"God, I know you gave me these songs and if I do say so myself Lord, you did a good job. These songs are good! How come more people aren't hearing them? Here I am, dragging my family to yet another small church in the middle of nowhere. Will we always struggle financially? I'm Your boy, God! What is the deal?"

Then I heard the still, small voice of the Holy Spirit say:

"David, I hear you and I know you and I know where you are. I am going to open up doors for ministry for you that you haven't even dreamed of, much less dared to ask me to open. However, when I open them, you are going to be so in love with Me that those doors won't be too important to you."

Those words once again reminded me of why I was doing what I did. I would love to tell you that that has been the only reminder I have needed, but alas, at times I forget all too easily.

Rita and I were at an artist retreat in Lindale, Texas sponsored by Melody Green (the wife of the late Keith Green.) Keith and Melody had started these week-long gatherings of recording artists and songwriters years earlier and Melody had continued them after Keith's death.

About 60 or 70 musicians and spouses gathered at Melody's ranch in a beautiful old house called "Father Heart". It was so invigorating to be with people who could understand some of the unique situations that us artist types found ourselves in.

We ate well, laughed a lot and forged some wonderful friendships with people like Steve and Marijean Green, Dallas and Linda Holm, early pioneers of contemporary Christian Music like the Second Chapter of Acts, Barry McGuire and other CCM artists including Steven Curtis Chapman and his wife Meribeth.

Paul Baloche, Jamie Owens-Collins, Kelly Willard and others including me led worship at times. You haven't lived until you sing standing next to Matthew Ward of Second Chapter of Acts. The man is a human synthesizer.

We also listened to powerful speakers like Winkie Pratney, (the world's oldest teen-ager), who was a brilliant biology student studying to be a chemist when God changed his heart and his plans. John Dawson, author of "Healing America's Wounds" who is now president of the worldwide youth movement "Youth With A Mission" was another of our favorite speakers.

A man named David Garrett from New Zealand was speaking at one of the sessions. David and his wife Dale pioneered the early "Praise and Worship" music movement that has swept the earth by simply putting Scripture verses to contemporary music.

The acclaim of those humble recordings, "Scripture in Song", inspired Maranatha Music and Hosanna Integrity to record and distribute "live" congregational worship.

As David finished speaking in the cozy living room at Father Heart, he encouraged us to listen to the Holy Spirit and if we had something to share with someone in the group, to feel free to quietly do so. Several moved around the room and engaged in quiet, encouraging conversation.

David Garrett, whom I had just met in that retreat, came to me and whispered in my ear: "David, your identity is not in your gifts, not in your songs, but it is found in who you are in Christ."

He was right on the mark, but in an example of how much I needed to be reminded of that, I protested inwardly:

"I know that- why is he telling me this, hasn't he heard some of my songs?"

Immediately my reaction was to try to validate my worth by bringing up (to myself) the songs I had written- exactly what he had just warned me about doing!

When I was an awkward teenager, unsure of myself, almost paralyzed by self-consciousness in social situations, I took comfort in my giftedness.

As I mentioned earlier, at high school parties I would be a wallflower; hiding on the edge of the crowd, hesitant to engage anyone in conversation. Several times, much to my secret delight, a friend would notice me and urge me to sit down at a piano and play and sing. Feigning humble reluctance, I would make my way to the keyboard and begin to play and sing. Before very long a crowd would gather and I would have my "fifteen minutes of fame."

I underwent a transformation from the wall to the piano. Why? Because though I lacked self-confidence, I knew that music was one of my strengths, so I leaned into, and unfortunately found my identity in my gifts, instead of just being who I was.

When I was converted to Christ, for years I would unwittingly do the same thing-albeit with slightly different terminology. Instead of being talented, now I was called "blessed". Instead of sounding good I was called "anointed of the Holy Spirit." But the principle was the same. On the stage in front of an audience I knew how to play and sing from the heart- I knew how to be real in that environment.

Once off the platform, however, I reverted back to being a self-conscious people pleaser. I said what I thought people wanted to hear because I was still desperately afraid of being rejected and unsure of who I was in Christ.

Paradoxically it was when I was at my lowest point in our marriage struggles, when I had no energy to sing or play or perform for others, that I realized that God really did love me for me; not for what I did or what I could do for Him!

I also began to be set free to be the real me- and I am coming to really know and love who I am.

I am thankful that most of the time my shortcomings have been exposed privately between me and the Lord- although it is important for me to have some safe people in my life to be totally transparent with.

Sometimes after finishing writing a new song I have smugly thought, "People sure need to hear that!"- only to hear the Lord say "You need to hear it more than they do, why do you think I gave the song to you first!"

As with many lessons learned, my challenge is to keep the pendulum in the middle- to not put too much value on the gifts, yet not put too little either. True humility is to have an accurate assessment of Who God is and who I am. With humility comes the proper perspective… and gratitude.

I am grateful for the discipline of the Lord. There is a wonderful verse in the Bible that says: *"All discipline for the present seems not to be joyful, but sorrowful, nevertheless for those who have been trained by it, it yields the peaceful fruit of righteousness.* (1 Peter 1:6)

My heavenly Father God has been patient and loving and kind to me, helping me to grow, reminding me to keep my priorities in order and graciously picking me up when I fall.

Rejoice not against me oh mine enemy. When I fall, I shall arise. When I sit in darkness, the Lord shall be a light unto me. (Micah 7:8 KJV)

-19-
Free

Most studio musicians I know are very clever and funny. I particularly love when we take a lunch break together and the hilarious stories start. One guitar player told of a drummer friend who had just joined James Brown's road band. After a few frenzied rehearsals to teach the new drummer the songs, it was time to go on tour.

James Brown was notorious for his unique, colloquial communication methods. Early in the tour, during a funky song, James turned around to the drummer and made a move with his hand like he was shaking paint off of a paintbrush. He yelled to the new guy: "Tang the hump!"

The new drummer didn't understand what the godfather of soul was telling him so he mouthed the question, "What?"

Again, the paintbrush motion and "tang the hump."

After another such exchange, the drummer finally realized that James Brown was telling him to hit the bell part of the cymbal- the "hump" which, when struck that way, made a distinctive "tanging" sound!

Rita could be a joker herself. Once we were traveling to a concert with her brother Dave and we stopped for the night in a motel. We were newlyweds and Dave must have been about 16 years old. We got one motel room with two double beds; it was late so we got ready for bed.

Rita and I had been fussing with each other about something that has long been forgotten, nothing major, just a newlywed spat.

I went into the bathroom to brush my teeth and while I was doing that, I started to feel bad about my part in our argument. When I came back into the bedroom the lights were turned off so I crawled into bed and snuggled up to Rita, whispering in my bride's ear just how sorry I was for our fight.

Just before I tenderly kissed her cheek I heard someone howling with laughter. Dave threw off the covers and my face turned red as a beet. Rita and Dave had switched beds and I almost smooched my brother-in-law!

The Bible says that "laughter does good like a medicine". I laugh as I remember the time I went to a radio interview at a predominately African American station in Gary, Indiana that played my music. When I walked in the control room to meet the DJ that had invited me, his jaw dropped when he saw that I was a white guy.

He said "I thought you was a brother, you sounded like a brother!" He didn't know what a compliment he had just paid me.

I am grateful for what I have gained from the celebratory, passionate spirit of African Americans. I am reminded of a story about the slaves in the fields, singing what must have sounded like an obscure lyric to the passersby:

"Just over by the big oak tree, heading for the Northern Star, when the river takes a winding turn, you will know where you are." There were other such mysterious words that, when all put together, was a map of the Underground Railroad. These slaves were singing the way to their freedom!

Another story is of a young slave girl that was treated harshly by her master. She was forbidden to speak, to sing, or to do anything that the master didn't want her to do. She lived a life of fear and soon succumbed to hopelessness about her fate.

Her master decided to sell her while she was still young and strong enough to fetch a good price. This young lady, stripped of her dignity and most of her clothes, was chained hand and foot and put on the auction block to be gawked at, ridiculed and sold.

A well dressed, wealthy man walks into town and saw the girl who was about to be sold. He went to the auctioneer and asked about the girl. The auctioneer, seeing that the man was rich, doubled the price he had originally intended to ask. The man paid the fee and approached the young slave girl, who trembled as he came near to her.

"Young lady, I have paid the price for your freedom. You are free to go."

As he reached for the shackles around the woman's hands, she flinched. She had rarely experienced touch that was not brutal and abusive.

"You don't have to be afraid of me; I have purchased your freedom. You can go anywhere you want to go."

A lifetime of mistreatment is not alleviated by a few nice words, yet the young lady couldn't deny that hope seemed to be rising in her. She mumbled: "C-can I go anywhere I want to g-go?"

"Yes, and you can say anything you want to say."

The slave thought about the days when she had to sing in a bucket so the cruel master wouldn't hear her and punish her. The kindly gentleman finished taking the shackles off of her hands and knelt down to unloose the chains around her scarred, worn, bare feet.

He said, "You can do anything you want to do, I have set you free."

He finished loosening the chains around her feet, stood up and looked at the frightened girl. The man smiled; it was a genuinely friendly smile, not the smile of someone who was out to take advantage of her.

Swallowing hard, she asked him, "Can I really do anything I want to do?"

The answer came: "Yes."

"Can I really say anything that I want to say?"

Laughing softly, the man replied, "Yes, and you can go anywhere you want to go."

Free of the chains, the young lady faced the one who had paid the price to win her release. She looked him in his kindly eyes and said the words that changed her life forever: "Then I want to go with you."

Sing Me Home

I have had a waking dream in which I was a frightened young boy being pursued by something, a ravenous wolf or other wild beast, through dense woods. I ran as fast as I could through the gathering twilight but my unknown pursuer was gaining on me. My face and arms and legs were scratched by the brambles and the branches and I was almost out of breath- but my fear kept me running.

Suddenly I came into a clearing where I saw a beautiful, welcoming, warmly lit home. I had no time to wonder who the home belonged to; I went to the door, praying that it wasn't locked. The doorknob turned, I pushed open the door and rushed inside. No sooner had I entered than a kindly man that I instinctively knew was my heavenly Father smiled at me and held me in His strong embrace.

He lovingly bathed my wounds and clothed me with a fresh robe. My Father prepared a wonderful meal for me. I was safe, I was whole, I was home.

That waking dream inspired this chorus:

Sing me home Lord sing me home.
When the night gets dark and the journey gets long
I can find my way if I hear Your song
Oh Father sing me home
Oh Father sing me home.

Once in an individual counseling session, the psychologist and I talked about my anxiety level. "On a scale of 1 to 10, what number would you give to your usual state of being- with 1 being that you feel totally at peace and 10 being very anxious and afraid?"

After thinking about it for a bit, (it has been hard for me to instantly access what I am feeling), I replied: "Usually my anxiety level is at a 4 or 5."

With an understanding look my counselor said, "When someone has experienced the trauma of being sexually abused as a child they learn to live "on alert"; their intensity and anxiety level is much higher, even in non-threatening situations, than people who have not experienced that trauma. It also takes a tremendous amount of energy to stay at that level- that's one reason abuse victims are easily tired and depressed."

It made sense to hear that. It made me sad to hear that. It made me angry to hear that. The therapist then began to teach me some breathing techniques and other exercises to bring my anxiety level down.

There is a passage in the Bible that talks about the "renewing of our minds." It takes time and practice to change old patterns of thinking.

I relate to myself differently than I used to. I relate to God, to Rita and my family differently now. I am more trusting and more at peace. I also have more emotional and spiritual energy to be creative. The songs are flowing and I have been very blessed.

Do I still get anxious at times? Of course I do, but again I find encouragement in the Word of God: "When I am afraid I will trust in You.

"When my anxious thoughts multiply within me, your consolations, O Lord, delight my soul."

One of my favorite things about Jesus the Jazz Preacher is that He frees me to be the person I was born to be. He says:

"Whom the Son sets free is free indeed."

After a conference in Roanoke, VA I was driving the eight hour trip home to Nashville. I was talking to God about some fears and needs and hopes I had. He began to answer me by giving me songs. I feverishly began to write down what I was hearing. Taking heavenly dictation while trying to keep my eyes on the road, I wrote four complete songs and a chorus on that trip home. Here is one song that I heard Him sing to me:

"Free"
David Baroni/ Bridge Building Music/ BMI/ CCLI

You didn't see Me coming
'Cause I've been right here all along
But you couldn't hear My music
While you sang your own song
And though the crowds applauded you felt strangely alone
But I've set you free to worship Me
And make My glory known
You're set free to leave your past behind you
Set free, from the chains that used to bind you
So spread your wings in worship like a new butterfly

Like an eagle to the sky
You are free indeed for I have set you free
By my blood through my Spirit
Those who make Me Lord of all
Can live inside My holy Presence
'Cause I've broken down the walls
And in your ordinary lives, my extraordinary grace
Will transform you to My image
As those set free behold My face

You're set free to leave your past behind you
Set free, from the chains that used to bind you
So spread your wings in worship like a new butterfly
Like an eagle to the sky
You are free indeed for I have set you free!

Words have power. God created the universe (which means "one word") with His words.

Music is powerful. Emotional defenses are dissolved by the right melody, chords and rhythm. When you combine words and music that are inspired by, and given life by, the Spirit of the Creator, the song is a living thing, affecting all who listen with the heart.

-20-
A Wonderful Life

Australia is a long journey from Nashville. It is about as far as one can travel around the world without heading back where you started if you kept going. Our oldest daughter Bethany lived in Newcastle, Australia for almost 2 years working with Youth With a Mission. While there Bethany met a young man from England named Benjamin Ian Nicholson. Their friendship blossomed into courtship, and now they are married. They live close to us here in Franklin, and Rita and I wouldn't be surprised to hear news of the coming patter of little feet any time now.

Charity, whom we refer to as our middle child, (though she preceded twin sister Celeste by only 9 minutes), is living in the Green Hills area of Nashville where she is a dance instructor and a dancer.

Celeste is currently living in Athens, Greece where she is helping teach at a school for refugee children. Her sister Charity did the same thing a year or so ago, and was so positively impacted by the experience that I think it rubbed off on Celeste.

Though the twins have a lot in common, they are also distinct and different persons- with very different personalities. I have enjoyed watching them grow into strong, beautiful individuals who also love their "twin-connection."

Rita and I are so grateful that our daughters and son-in-law all love each other and love life and love God.

One of my favorite films is Frank Capra's classic "It's A Wonderful Life", starring Jimmy Stewart and Donna Read. It has become one of our favorite family Christmas traditions to drink hot chocolate, eat some holiday cookies, and watch that movie together.

The story of Bedford Falls' George Bailey, and the way his life touched so many other lives around him, is a marvelous illustration of poet John Donne's observation that "no man is an island."

As I rehearse the comings and goings, the tapestry of my life so far; I can't help but think fondly about the wonderful friends that Rita and I have made- from places as far-flung as Kuwait and Italy, to our backyard here in Franklin.

We have stayed in people's homes and nice hotels, we have lodged in our share of dumps and less than idyllic locales as well; the 4 star hotels are comfortable and wonderful, but most of the best stories come from the more rustic settings.

In telling my story as it is thus far, I can't help but be reminded of the friends, mentors, encouragers that I have met along the way. I am amazed at how the pieces fit together.

Had Louis Baroni and Marjorie Rushing never met, I wouldn't be here. If I hadn't gone to USM, I wouldn't have met the members of Fancy Music. I wouldn't have moved to Jackson, Mississippi and therefore would not have moved to Muscle Shoals, Alabama. Kentucky Fried Chicken would just be another fast food restaurant had I not met my future wife there.

If Kent Henry had not invited me to a retreat where I met songwriters John Chisum and George Searcy, I would not have started writing songs at Bethel, and not become the worship pastor there. I would not have been a writer for Integrity Music, or a part of the International Worship Institute. Ben and Bethany would not have met for there would be no Bethany- or Charity or Celeste for that matter.

Is it Intelligent Design or random fate? I'm convinced that there is a God, and that He is lovingly involved in the weaving of the tapestry of our lives.

I am grateful for the people I have met like Nick and Caroline Coetzee from South Africa. Musically, Nick and I are twin sons of different mothers and have created several wonderful songs and CDs- he with his South African rhythms and melodies and unique acoustic guitar playing; me with my Mississippi Mud bass guitar and jazz and rhythm and blues influenced keyboard and vocals.

I have written songs with Canadians and Africans, like South African Erik Eskelund, who along with his wife Tami now pastor in Cape Cod. I love to go to Nigeria with my friend Wale Adenuga. I have written several songs there with Kunzle Fadahunsi- he is a delightful brother and is as fun as saying his name!

Some of our dear friends are Gail Stathis and Brian Van Deventer who are based in Greece with a far-reaching ministry called Europe and the Middle East, or Enabling Mission Endeavors (EME.) I cherish a photograph of my daughter Charity and me at sunset with the beautiful harbor of Mykonos Island in the background.

We have met precious people from Nigeria to Indonesia, Germany to Italy, where I was introduced to the homeland of my father's father by our dear friends Mike and Loretta Hopkins, who are missionaries based in Rome.

We have made friends from the Bahamas to Kuwait, and in Singapore, Austria, Belgium, Sweden, the Philippines, Canada and all over America.

In a way, each of us is George Bailey, every life touches so may other lives whether we are intentional about it or not. I am grateful to the people who have encouraged me in my journey; some are virtual strangers that I have met perhaps one time, but the words, notes, and smiles that they had for me were like food and drink that have helped sustain me on my journey.

Then there are those lifetime friends; too many for me to mention here, but I trust that you know who you are, and how thankful I am for you.

The Mississippi River has humble, stream-like origins in Minnesota. The "river" is so narrow it can be stepped over. As it is joined by other tributaries and rivers on the journey from north to south; past St. Louis and Memphis and Natchez, through Mark Twain country and the birthplace of the blues; the Mississippi becomes mighty: "Old Man River". The pristine stream becomes a non-stoppable water force that carries boats and barges and paddle-wheel steamboats on its substantial currents.

Life is like a river, friendships and family are tributaries that bring vital replenishing and fresh water.

Life is a tapestry, and each experience and each person we connect with, however tenuously or strongly, is part of an unbelievably beautiful work of art.

Life is a symphony and every person has vital notes or chords or percussion sounds that contribute to the masterpiece.

Life is also a Song.

There is a psalm that says *"The Lord is my strength and my song, He has become my salvation."*

I am a singer. Jesus is *the* Singer. I have a song. He *is* the Song. In a wonderful paradox, Jesus the Messenger is the Message, the Singer is the Song.

"I Don't Play the Music"
David Baroni/ Kingdomsongs Inc./ BMI/ CCLI

I don't play the music, the music's playing me
It's not my song I'm singing
He's the love song singing me
I am just an instrument in the Master's loving hands
It's not I but Christ Who lives, Oh I hope you understand

I don't write the lyrics, His Word is rewriting me
And when you look into my eyes
I hope you don't see just me
Don't think of me as humble
Don't think of me at all
'Cause my reasonable service to the Servant King
Is to give all that I am
To the One Who is my everything and

I don't play the music, the music's playing me
It's not my song I'm singing
He's the love song singing me
I am just an instrument in the Master's loving hands
It's not I but Christ Who lives
I pray you understand

I have tried improving, tried desperately to change
And though I wore a holy face, my selfish heart remained
When I came to my conclusion
Then the real me came to life
I finally started living on the day that I died
And any other life is just a lie
That's why I sing

I don't play the music, the music's playing me
It's not my song I'm singing
He's the love song singing me
I am just an instrument in the Master's loving hands
It's not I but Christ Who lives
I think you understand

An older preacher friend of mine, when complimented on his preaching, smiles and says, "Oh, I'm just a ditch that the water flows through." I know what he means, and in one way I agree with him; after all, Jesus said "Without Me you can do nothing."

However God is not interested in us for mere utilitarian purposes. We are far more than "ditches" to Him. Each one of us has a unique personality that Jesus frees us to express and enjoy. To me being set free to be myself is one of the best things about the gospel.

No Ways Tired

I have a recurring daydream about the latter years of my life. I envision sitting in a rocking chair on a porch overlooking a green field (maybe on a golf course!) as the sun sets through the trees.

Rita, the loving companion of my youth, is sitting beside me in another rocker. We are in our nineties and we are holding hands, not saying a word, but enjoying the easy silence in each others' company.

We share a lifetime of memories between us: wonderful adventures, precious times with our children, grandchildren and great grandchildren, God's grace through some storms and dark

143.

times, and the treasures of friendship from all over the world.

 We look into each others eyes and smile at the depth of love that we each see in the other. Life is good, I am at peace and I don't feel no ways tired.

I don't feel no ways tired
I don't feel no ways tired
O the Lord my Lord is the strength of me and
I don't feel no ways tired

About the Author

David Baroni is an internationally known songwriter, singer, musician, producer, arranger, conference speaker, recording artist and worship leader. He is the proud father of three wonderful daughters-Bethany, Charity and Celeste. David has been a songwriter with Integrity Music and is the president of KingdomSongs Inc. David and his wife, Rita, have ministered in 20 nations and 49 states.

David's solo piano series, "FingerPaintings", is highly regarded by many for its innovation and spirituality. His songs have been recorded by Ron Kenoly, Alvin Slaughter, Kent Henry, Don Moen, Selah, Morris Chapman, Phil Driscoll, Debby Boone, The Imperials, Natalie Grant, and many others.

Perhaps best known for his thoughtful, well crafted lyrics and prophetic, intuitive keyboard playing, David combines a childlike exuberance for Christ with the maturity of a seasoned minister of the Gospel. David has been on the faculty of the International Worship Institute for the past 13 years, (the past five years as Music Director), and is a member of The Gate in Nashville TN. He lives with his wife Rita in Franklin TN.

To order David's music, books and teaching CD's, or for bookings visit www.davidbaroni.com or email: david@davidbaroni.com

Godrest and Godspeed

Printed in the United States
132180LV00003B/4/P